THE HISTORY OF RUSSIA TO 1801

SOCIETIES AND CULTURES
RUSSIA

THE HISTORY OF RUSSIA TO 1801

EDITED BY ROSINA BECKMAN

Britannica®
Educational Publishing
IN ASSOCIATION WITH
ROSEN
EDUCATIONAL SERVICES

Published in 2019 by Britannica Educational Publishing (a trademark of Encyclopædia Britannica, Inc.) in association with The Rosen Publishing Group, Inc.
29 East 21st Street, New York, NY 10010

Distributed exclusively by Rosen Publishing.
To see additional Britannica Educational Publishing titles, go to rosenpublishing.com.

First Edition

Britannica Educational Publishing
J.E. Luebering: Executive Director, Core Editorial
Andrea R. Field: Managing Editor, Compton's by Britannica

Rosen Publishing
Amelie von Zumbusch: Editor
Nelson Sá: Art Director
Brian Garvey: Series Designer/Book Layout
Cindy Reiman: Photography Manager
Nicole Baker: Photo Researcher

Library of Congress Cataloging-in-Publication Data

Names: Beckman, Rosina, editor.
Title: The history of Russia to 1801 / edited by Rosina Beckman.
Description: New York : Britannica Educational Publishing, in Association with Rosen Educational Services, 2019. | Series: Societies and cultures : Russia |
Includes bibliographical references and index. | Audience: Grades 7–12.
Identifiers: LCCN 2017047204| ISBN 9781538301821 (library bound : alk. paper)
| ISBN 9781538301838 (pbk. : alk. paper)
Subjects: LCSH: Russia—History.
Classification: LCC DK39 .H57 2019 | DDC 947—dc23
LC record available at https://lccn.loc.gov/2017047204

Manufactured in the United States of America

Photo credits: Cover, pp. 3, 20, 32, 38-39, 67, 89, 107 Heritage Images/Hulton Fine Art Collection/Getty Images; cover and interior pages (flag) fckncg/Shutterstock.com; cover and interior pages (emblem) N-sky/iStock/Thinkstock; p. 9 © Photos.com/Thinkstock; p. 14 Time & Life Pictures/The LIFE Picture Collection/Getty Images; pp. 17, 102 © Encyclopaedia Britannica, Inc.; pp. 24, 73, 82 Heritage Images/Hulton Archive/Getty Images; p. 29 Sovfoto/Universal Images Group/Getty Images; p. 41 © Courtesy of the trustees of the British Museum. Photograph, J.R. Freeman & Co. Ltd.; p. 44 © The National Museum of Denmark, Department of Ethnography; p. 47 DEA/A. Dagli Orti/De Agostini/Getty Images; p. 53 Franz Marc Frei/Lonely Planet Images/Getty Images; pp. 57, 100 Universal History Archive/Universal Images Group/Getty Images; pp. 60, 110 © Courtesy of the State Historical Museum, Moscow; p. 71 © Courtesy of the Rijksmuseum. Object no. SK-A-116; p. 77 Print Collector/Hulton Archive/Getty Images; p. 86 DEA/W. Buss/De Agostini/Getty Images; p. 91 Art Gallery, Tver, Russia/Bridgeman Images; p. 93 Universal Images Group/Getty Images; p. 97 Courtesy of the Rijksmuseum, Amsterdam (SK-A-1929); p. 114 Fine Art Images/SuperStock/Getty Images.

CONTENTS

INTRODUCTION

The land that is now Russia has been inhabited since the second millennium BCE. Slavic peoples originally lived over a large area of eastern Europe that included parts of what are now Poland, Ukraine, and Belarus. In the 5th and 6th centuries CE the Slavs spread south and east, some of them into southern Russia.

In about 830 traders from Scandinavia moved into the north Volga region. These traders were known as the Rus—the source of the name Russia. Soon the Rus and other Scandinavian groups—together called the Varangians—extended their raiding down the main river routes toward the Middle East.

According to tradition, the Slavs of Novgorod, tired of political turmoil, invited the Varangian prince Rurik to rule the city. Rurik's successor Oleg added Kiev to his domains, making it his capital. This was the beginning of Kievan Rus, the first East Slavic state. In time Kievan Rus was crushed by the onslaught of the Mongols. Asian customs became a part of Russian culture, but as long as they paid tribute the Russians were free to practice their religion and native customs.

Mongol rule was eventually undercut by internal discord. The principality of Muscovy (Moscow), nestled deep in the forest at the hub of the major trade routes, developed at the expense of the Mongols as their power declined. As descendants of the Rurik line, Muscovite princes came to be regarded by the people as justified leaders of all Russians. The best-known ruler of Rurikid Muscovy is Ivan IV, called "the Terrible" because of his savage cruelty. He was followed first by his mentally unfit son Fyodor and then by Fyodor's brother-in-law Boris Godunov. After Godunov's death in 1605, Russia descended into civil war. This unsettled period ended with Michael Romanov's election as tsar in 1613, launching the Romanov Dynasty.

The Russian Empire—and with it the beginning of modern Russian history—dates from the reign of Peter the Great (1682–1725). Peter defeated Sweden in the Second Northern War (Great Northern War) and gained an outlet to the Baltic Sea. He founded a navy, introduced factories, reformed the administrative machinery, and organized a modern army. He forced education upon his officers and members of his court, many of whom could

Peter the Great disguised himself as a ship's carpenter while traveling through western Europe in 1697–98. What he learned helped his efforts to make Russia a modern power in the western European world.

not read. He created a new Russian capital—St. Petersburg—on the Gulf of Finland.

Although Peter died in 1725, his work survived almost half a century of incompetent rulers. Then Catherine the Great came to the throne in 1762. She again took up the task of reform. She also greatly expanded the Russian Empire. Her armies defeated Turkey, giving Russia control of the northern Black Sea coast and the Crimean Peninsula. During her reign Russia also acquired vast amounts of territory from Poland.

CHAPTER ONE

THE EARLY RUS AND THE MONGOL PERIOD

Indo-European, Ural-Altaic, and diverse other peoples have occupied what is now the territory of Russia since the 2nd millennium BCE, but little is known about them. In ancient times, Greek and Iranian settlements appeared in the southernmost portions of what is now Ukraine. Trading empires of that era seem to have known and exploited the northern forests—particularly the vast triangular-shaped region west of the Urals between the Kama and Volga rivers—but these contacts had little lasting impact. Between the 4th and 9th centuries CE, the Huns, Avars, Goths, and Magyars passed briefly over the same terrain, but these transitory occupations also had little influence upon the East Slavs, who during this time were spreading south and east from an area between the Elbe River and the Pripet Marshes. In the 9th century, as a result of penetration into the area from the north and south by northern European and Middle Eastern merchant adventurers, their society was exposed to new economic, cultural, and political forces.

THE RISE OF THE RUS

From about 770 to about 830, commercial explorers began an intensive penetration of the Volga region. From early bases in the estuaries of the rivers of the eastern Baltic region, Germanic commercial-military bands, probably in search of new routes to the east, began to penetrate territory populated by Finnic and Slavic tribes, where they found amber, furs, honey, wax, and timber products. The indigenous population offered little resistance to their incursions, and there was no significant local authority to negotiate the balance between trade, tribute, and plunder. From the south, trading organizations based in northern Iran and North Africa, seeking the same products, and particularly slaves, became active in the lower Volga, the Don, and, to a lesser extent, the Dnieper region. The history of the Khazar state is intimately connected with these activities.

About 830, commerce appears to have declined in the Don and Dnieper regions. There was increased activity in the north Volga, where Scandinavian traders who had previously operated from bases on Lakes Ladoga and Onega established a new centre, near present-day Ryazan. There, in this period, the first nominal ruler of Rus (called, like the Khazar emperor, khagan) is mentioned by Islamic and Western sources. This Volga Rus khagan state may be considered the first direct political antecedent of the Kievan state.

Within a few decades these Rus, together with other Scandinavian groups operating farther west, extended their raiding activities down the main river routes toward Baghdad and Constantinople, reaching the latter in 860. The Scandinavians involved in these exploits are known as Varangians; they were adventurers of diverse origins, often led by princes of warring dynastic clans. One of these princes, Rurik, is considered the progenitor of the dynasty that ruled in various portions of East Slavic territory until 1598. Evidences of the Varangian expansion are particularly clear in the coin hoards of 900–930. The number of Middle Eastern coins reaching northern regions, especially Scandinavia, indicates a flourishing trade. Written records tell of Rus raids upon Constantinople and the northern Caucasus in the early 10th century.

In the period from about 930 to 1000, the region came under complete control by Varangians from Novgorod. This period saw the development of the trade route from the Baltic to the Black Sea, which established the basis of the economic life of the Kievan principality and determined its political and cultural development.

The degree to which the Varangians may be considered the founders of the Kievan state has been hotly debated since the 18th century. The debate has from the beginning borne nationalistic overtones. Recent works by Russians have generally minimized or ignored the role of the Varangians, while non-Russians have occasionally

Rurik's story is told in the 12th-century Russian Primary Chronicle *but is not accepted at face value by modern historians. This is an artist's idea of what the semilegendary founder of the Rurik dynasty looked like.*

exaggerated it. Whatever the case, the lifeblood of the sprawling Kievan organism was the commerce organized by the princes. To be sure, these early princes were not "Swedes" or "Norwegians" or "Danes;" they thought in categories not of nation but of clan. But they certainly were not East Slavs. There is little reason to doubt the predominant role of the Varangian Rus in the creation of the state to which they gave their name.

KIEV

The consecutive history of the first East Slavic state begins with Prince Svyatoslav (died 972). His victorious campaigns against other Varangian centres, the Khazars, and the Volga Bulgars and his intervention in the Byzantine-Danube Bulgar conflicts of 968–971 mark the full hegemony of his clan in Rus and the emergence of a new political force in eastern Europe. But Svyatoslav was neither a lawgiver nor an organizer. It was his son Vladimir (c. 980–1015) who established the dynastic seniority system of his clan as the political structure by which the scattered territories of Rus were to be ruled. He invited or permitted the patriarch of Constantinople to establish an episcopal see in Rus.

Vladimir extended the realm (to include the watersheds of the Don, Dnieper, Dniester, Neman, Western Dvina, and upper Volga), destroyed or incorporated the remnants of competing Varangian organizations, and established relations with neighbouring dynasties. The successes of his long reign made it possible for the reign of his son Yaroslav (ruled 1019–54) to produce a flowering of cultural life. But neither Yaroslav, who gained control of Kiev only after a bitter struggle against his brother Svyatopolk (1015–19), nor his successors in Kiev were able to provide lasting political stability within the enormous realm. The political history of Rus is one of clashing separatist and centralizing trends inherent in the contradiction between local settlement and colonization on the one hand and the hegemony of the clan elder, ruling from Kiev, on the other. As Vladimir's 12 sons and innumerable grandsons prospered in the rapidly developing territories they inherited, they and their retainers acquired settled interests that conflicted both with one another and with the interests of unity.

The conflicts were not confined to Slavic lands: the Turkic nomads who moved into the southern steppe during the 11th century (first the Torks, later the Kipchaks—also known as the Polovtsy, or Cumans) got drawn in the constant internecine rivalries, and Rurikid and Turkic princes often fought on both sides. In 1097, representatives of the leading branches of the dynasty, along with their Turkic allies, met at Liubech, north of Kiev, and agreed to divide the Kievan territory among themselves and their descendants; later, however, Vladimir II Monomakh was briefly successful in reuniting the land of Rus (1113–25).

THE DECLINE OF KIEV

The hegemony of the prince of Kiev depended on the cohesion of the clan of Rurik and the relative importance

This map shows the extent of the state of Kievan Rus at its peak in the early to mid-11th century.

of the southern trade, both of which began to decline in the late 11th century. This decline seems to have been part of a general shift of trade routes associated with the First Crusade (1096–99) that made the route from the Black Sea to the Baltic less attractive to commerce. At the same time, conflicts among the Rurikid princes acquired a more pronounced regional and separatist nature, reflecting new patterns in export trade along the northern and western periphery. Novgorod, in particular, began to gravitate toward closer relations with the cities of the Hanseatic League, which controlled the Baltic trade. Smolensk, Polotsk, and Pskov became increasingly involved in trade along western land routes, while Galicia and Volhynia established closer links with Poland and Hungary. The princes of these areas still contested the crown of the "grand prince of Kiev and all of Rus," but the title became an empty one. When Andrew Bogolyubsky (Andrew I) of Suzdal won Kiev and the title in 1169, he sacked the city and returned to the upper Volga, apparently seeing no advantage in establishing himself in the erstwhile capital. (Roman Mstislavich of Galicia and Volhynia repeated these actions in 1203.) By the middle of the 12th century, the major principalities, owing to the prosperity and colonization of the Kievan period, had developed into independent political and economic units.

SOCIAL AND POLITICAL INSTITUTIONS

The paucity of evidence about social and political institutions in Kievan Rus suggests that they were rudimentary.

The East Slavs had no significant tradition of supratribal political organization before the coming of the Varangians, who themselves had little interest in institutions beyond those necessary for the exploitation of their rich, new territory. The territory of Rus, moreover, was immense and sparsely settled. The scattered towns, some probably little more than trading posts, were separated by large primeval forests and swamps.

Thus, although the campaigns of Svyatoslav indicate the political vacuum that his clan filled, he construed his domains as a clan possession rather than as a territorial or national state. His successor, Vladimir, however, seems to have been conscious of one political element—organized religion—that distinguished both the contemporary empires and the newly established principalities in Poland and Hungary from his own. The church provided the concepts of territorial and hierarchical organization that helped to make states out of tribal territories; its teachings transformed a charismatic prince into a king possessing the attributes and responsibilities of a national leader, judge, and first Christian of the realm.

Once Vladimir had adopted Christianity in 988, his rule was supported by the propagation of Byzantine notions of imperial authority. The political traditions and conditions of Rus, however, required that the actual workings of the political system and some of its style be derived from other sources. The succession system, probably a vestige of the experience of the Rus khaganate in the upper Volga, was based upon two principles: the indivisibility

This image of Vladimir I—known in full as Vladimir Svyatoslavich*—is from Saint Sophia Cathedral, in Kiev. The first Christian ruler in Kievan Rus, he is considered a saint.*

of the basic territory of Rus (the principalities of Kiev, Chernigov, and Pereyaslavl) and the shared sovereignty of a whole generation. Seniority passed through an ascension by stages from elder brother to younger and from the youngest eligible uncle to the eldest eligible nephew. Such a system was admirably suited to the needs of the dynasty, because, by providing a rotating advancement of members of the clan through apprenticeships in the various territories of the realm, it assured control of the key points of the far-flung trading network by princes who were subject to traditional sanctions, and it gave them experience in lands over which they could someday expect to rule from Kiev. This system served well for a century after it was given final form by Vladimir and was revived by Monomakh (Vladimir II, ruled 1113–25), but it could not survive the decline of Kiev's importance.

Individual Rurikid princes maintained military retinues led by boyars. The princes and boyars drew their most significant revenues from the tribute or taxes collected annually in kind from territories under their control and disposed of in the export trade. Most of the population, apparently free peasants living in traditional agricultural communes, had little other connection with the dynasty.

Little is known of law in this period; it may be assumed that juridical institutions had not developed on a broad scale. The earliest law code (1016), called the "Russian Law," was one of the "Barbarian" law codes common throughout Germanic Europe. It dealt primarily with princely law—that is, with the fines to be imposed by the prince or his representative in the case of specified offenses.

Some scholars have held that, since land was in the hands of the boyar class, who exploited the labour of slaves and peasants, Kievan society should be termed feudal. The meagre sources indicate, however, that Kiev experienced nothing like the complex and highly regulated legal and economic relationships associated with feudalism in western Europe. Kiev's political system existed primarily for and by international trade in forest products and depended on a money economy in which the bulk of the population scarcely participated. The subsistence agriculture of the forest regions was not the source of Kiev's wealth, nor was it the matrix within which law and politics and history were made.

Formal culture came to Rus, along with Christianity, from the multinational Byzantine synthesis, primarily through South Slavic intermediaries. A native culture, expressed in a now-lost pagan ritual folklore and traditions in the arts and crafts, existed before the Kievan period and then persisted alongside the formal culture, but its influence on the latter is conjectural.

No single one of the regional (or, later, national) cultures, perhaps least of all that of Muscovy, can be called the heir of Kiev, although all shared the inheritance. The strands of continuity were everywhere strained, if not broken, in the period after Kiev's decline. But "Golden Kiev" was always present, in lore and bookish tradition, as a source of emulation and renascence.

THE LANDS OF RUS

The decline of Kiev led to regional developments so striking that the subsequent period has often been called the "Period of Feudal Partition." This phrase is misleading: "feudal" is hardly more applicable to the widely varying institutions of this time than to those of the Kievan period, and "partition" implies a former unity of which there is insufficient evidence.

NOVGOROD

Novgorod arose in the 9th century and remained the most important commercial centre of the Kievan period. The changes of the latter Kievan period did not diminish the town's importance, for it benefited both from the increased activity of the Hanseatic League and from the development of the upper Volga region, for which it was a major trade outlet. Although Novgorod was an early base for the Rurikids, the princely traditions characteristic of Kiev and other post-Kievan centres never developed there. When Kiev declined, Novgorod soon (1136) declared its independence from princely power, and, although it accepted princely protectors from various neighbouring dynasties, it remained a sovereign city until conquered by Muscovy (Moscow).

During the 13th century, Novgorod's burghers easily found an accommodation with the invading Mongols. In the Mongol period its energetic river pirates pushed farther north and east toward the Urals and even down the Volga, and Novgorod's prosperity was generally unbroken until the commercial revolution of the 16th century. Its absorption by the growing principality of Muscovy in 1478 ended its political independence and changed its social structure, but Novgorod's characteristic economic and cultural life did not end with that catastrophe.

Novgorod was governed by an oligarchy of great trading boyar families who controlled the exploitation of the hinterland. They chose (from among themselves) a

This manuscript recounts how Novgorod's defenders—led by Alexander Nevsky, prince of Vladimir—repulsed an attack by the Teutonic Knights on the ice of Lake Peipus in 1242.

mayor, a military commander, and a council of aldermen, who controlled the affairs of the city and its territories. The town itself was divided into five "ends," which seem to have corresponded to the "fifths" into which the hinterland was divided. There was in addition a *veche* (council), apparently a kind of town meeting of broad but indeterminate composition whose decisions, it would appear, were most often controlled by the oligarchy. A major role in politics was played by the archbishop, who after 1156 controlled the lands and incomes previously owned by the Kievan princes and who appears throughout Novgorod's history as a powerful, often independent figure.

THE NORTHWEST

During this period, much of the territory of the principalities of Smolensk, Polotsk, Turov, and Pinsk was controlled by the grand duchy of Lithuania, which was essentially an international or nonnational formation led by a foreign dynasty (of eastern Lithuanian pagan origins) ruling over predominantly Belarusian and Ukrainian populations. By the 15th century the dynasty had become Slavic in culture (a version of Belarusian was the official language of the realm), and at its height under Vytautas (1392–1430) it controlled all the old Kievan territory outside Russia proper—that is, most of present-day Lithuania, Belarus, Moldova, and Ukraine. In 1385 the grand duchy joined the kingdom of Poland, and the union was sealed shortly thereafter by the marriage of Grand Prince Jogaila to Jadwiga, the Polish queen.

THE NORTHEAST

The region bounded by the Oka and Volga rivers, later to be the heartland of the Grand Principality of Moscow, was settled before the arrival of Slavs from Novgorod and the Baltic area by a Finnic tribe. Rostov, the earliest princely centre, was from Vladimir's time included in the princely rotation system. In the 12th century it became the patrimony of the younger branch of Vladimir II Monomakh's family (who founded the new princely centre Vladimir in 1108). Under his son Yury Dolgoruky (1125–57) and grandson Andrew I (1157–74), the principality reached a high political and cultural development, which it retained through much of the succeeding century. Early in the 13th century the principality of Moscow was created as an appanage (royal grant) within the grand principality of Vladimir, and this new seat grew in importance when Michael Khorobrit, brother of Alexander Nevsky, conquered Vladimir (1248) and made himself prince of both centres. Daniel, Nevsky's son and the progenitor of all the later Rurikid princes of Moscow, had a long and successful reign (1276–1303), but at his death the principality still embraced little more than the territory of the present Moscow province. The beginning of Moscow's rise to its later preeminence came during the reign of Daniel's son Ivan (1328–41), who, by cooperating with Öz Beg, khan of the Golden Horde, and also by his shrewd purchases (probably of tax-farming rights), greatly expanded the influence of his principality.

THE SOUTHWEST

The lands of Galicia and Volhynia were always ethnically and economically distinct from the Kievan region proper, as well as from more distant regions. Agriculture was highly developed, and trade, particularly in the valuable local salt, tended to take westward and overland routes. Galicia, already a separate principality by 1100, grew as Kiev declined. Later, Roman Mstislavich of Volhynia (ruled 1199–1205) conquered Galicia and united the two principalities. Under his son Daniel (1201–64), difficulties with the Galician landed magnates and the interference of the Hungarians weakened the principality, and it was subjugated in 1240 by the Mongol invasion. Eventually this region came under the domination of Lithuania (Volhynia) and Poland (Galicia).

THE MONGOL PERIOD

In 1223, when the first Mongol reconnaissance into former Kievan territory led to the disastrous defeat of a Volhynian-Galician-Polovtsian army on the Kalka River, the Rurikid principalities had for generations been intermittently at war. Kiev was in ruins, Novgorod was preoccupied with commerce and with its northern neighbours, Galicia was being torn internally and drawn increasingly into Polish and Hungarian dynastic affairs, and Vladimir-Suzdal, apparently the leading principality, could not resist the finely organized and skillful mounted bowmen of the steppe, the greatest military force of the age.

Tradition has exaggerated both the destructiveness of the first Mongol conquests and the strength of the resistance. The Mongols aimed to revive, under a unified political system, the trade that had traditionally crossed the Central Asian steppe and vitalized the economy of the pastoral nomads. As they moved westward, they gained the collaboration of groups of Turkic nomads and the predominantly Iranian and Muslim traders in the towns of the old Silk Road; they encountered the greatest resistance in sedentary political centres and among landowning elites. The lands of the Rus presented numerous similarities with the Central Asian areas that the Mongols had already conquered. There too, a former commercial empire had fallen apart into an aggregation of warring principalities. There too, ready recruits were to be found—in the Polovtsians, who controlled the lower Dnieper and Volga and Don, and in the Muslim merchants, who dealt in the towns on the Crimean Peninsula and the upper Volga. These merchants showed the way, first (1223) to the Crimean Peninsula and up the Volga to the old centre of Bulgar, later to Ryazan, Rostov, and the Suzdalian towns, and still later (1240) to Kiev and Galicia.

Many of the conquered cities made a striking recovery and adjustment to the new relationships. Some towns, such as Kiev, never fully recovered in Mongol times, but the cities of the Vladimir-Suzdal region clearly prospered. New centres, such as Moscow and Tver, hardly mentioned in any source before the Mongol period, arose and flourished in Mongol times.

This 20th-century painting by an unknown Soviet artist shows members of the Golden Horde extracting tribute from conquered Russian townspeople.

Thus, the Mongol invasion was not everywhere a catastrophe. The local princely dynasties continued unchanged in their traditional seats; some princes resisted the new authority and were killed in battle, but no alien princes ever became established in Slavic territory. Few Mongols remained west of the Urals after the conquest; political and fiscal administration was entrusted to the same Turkic clan leaders and Islamic merchants who had for generations operated in the area. The whole of the Novgorodian north remained outside the sphere of direct Tatar control, although the perspicacious burghers maintained correct relations with the khans.

TATAR RULE

After a brief attempt to revive the ancient centres of Bulgar and Crimea, the Jucids (the family of Jöchi, son of Genghis Khan, who inherited the western portion of his empire) established a new capital, Itil. (It was moved to New Sarai, near the site of Tsaritsyn, modern Volgograd, about 1260.) These towns became the commercial and administrative centres of what was later to be called the "Golden Horde" (the term is probably a Western invention). Its East Slavic territories were tributaries of an extensive empire, including, at its height, Crimea, the Polovtsian steppe from the Danube to the Ural River, the former territories of the Bulgar empire (including the fur-rich Mordvinian forests and parts of western Siberia), and in Asia the former kingdom of Khwārezm, including Urgench, the cultural capital of the Jucids. Control of the Slavic lands was exercised through the native princes, some of whom spent much of their time at the Mongol capital, and through agents charged with overseeing the activities of the princes and particularly the fiscal levies.

This multinational commercial empire was unstable. Early in the history of the Golden Horde, the khans of Sarai, who tended to reflect the interests of the Volga tribes, were challenged by the tribal princes of the west, whose control of the Danube, Bug, and Dnieper routes and of the access to Crimea gave them considerable political and economic power. As early as 1260, Nokhai, one of these western chieftains, showed his independence of Sarai by establishing his own foreign policy, and toward the end of the 13th century he seized control of Sarai itself. At his death the eastern tribes reestablished their control in Sarai, but, in the reign of the great Öz Beg (1313–41), the high point of Golden Horde power, the west was again ascendant. Öz Beg based his power upon firm control of Crimea and had extensive relations with the Genoese and Venetians, who controlled the main ports there. After the death of Öz Beg's son Jani Beg in 1357, however, the empire began to reveal serious internal strains. The tribes of the west paid little heed to the dizzying succession of khans in Sarai. The northern Russian princes focused on maneuvering for their own advantage in the internecine politics of the Golden Horde. The Volga Bulgar region was detached by a dissident Tatar prince, while the lands of the east were drawn into the orbit of the Turkic conqueror Timur (Tamerlane).

The Golden Horde's last cycle of integration and dismemberment was linked with events in Timur's domains. Tokhtamysh, son of a minor Tatar prince, had been unsuccessfully involved in the skirmishes around the throne of Sarai in the 1370s and had fled to the court of Timur, with whose aid he returned to Sarai and vanquished the tribal leaders who had opposed him. Having defeated and made peace with them, he now turned to defeat Mamai (1381), who had the previous year been defeated by Prince Dmitry Donskoy (grand prince of Moscow, 1359–89). Mamai's western tribal allies went over to Tokhtamysh, and, for a brief time, the major components of the tribal structure

This illustration shows Tokhtamysh's invasion of Moscow in 1382. Tokhtamysh sacked and burned Moscow in retaliation for the Russians' victory over the Golden Horde at the Battle of Kulikovo in 1380.

of the Golden Horde were reunited. Tokhtamysh successfully attacked Moscow (just as Mamai had hoped to do) and set about consolidating his gains. As his power grew, however, Tokhtamysh was drawn into a struggle with Timur, who had conquered much of Iran, the south Caucasus, and eastern Anatolia. After a number of encounters in the northern Caucasus, Timur, who apparently was intent upon diversion of east-west trade through his own Transoxanian and north Iranian territories, set out to destroy Tokhtamysh and the latter's commercial centres. In 1395–96 Timur's armies systematically annihilated Sarai, Azov, and Kaffa. The Golden Horde never recovered.

THE RISE OF MUSCOVY

From the beginning of the Tatar period, the Rurikid princes displayed much disunity. During the reign of Öz Beg there was a shift of alignments. The princes of Moscow and their allies, together with Öz Beg and his Crimean supporters, generally opposed the princes of Tver, Pskov, and, intermittently, Novgorod. The major punitive measures directed by Öz Beg against Tver with Muscovite support were a part of this pattern.

The links forged in the 14th century between Moscow and Crimea (and Sarai, while Öz Beg controlled it) were crucial to Moscow's later preeminence. They not only afforded Moscow a steady and profitable export trade for its furs but, because of contacts between Crimean merchants and Byzantium, also led to close relations between the Muscovite hierarchy and the patriarchate of Constantinople. This special relationship was but one of the reasons for the eventual rise of Moscow as leader of the Russian lands. Situated in the northeast, linked with all of the major navigable river systems and with the steppe, close to the major fur-producing regions and the most intensely settled agricultural lands, served by a succession of shrewd and long-lived princes, Moscow came naturally to a position of preeminence during the 14th century and was best equipped to enter the struggle for the political inheritance of the Golden Horde that followed the destruction of its capitals by Timur.

CULTURAL LIFE AND THE "TATAR INFLUENCE"

Traditional scholarship advanced the notions that (1) the Mongol invasion "destroyed" Kievan culture, (2) the Tatar period was one of "stultification" and "isolation from the West," and (3) "Russian" culture was deeply influenced by Golden Horde culture, in particular by "Oriental" conceptions of despotism. These views do not accord with the evidence and should probably be discarded.

First, Kievan culture was not destroyed. In the shift of the cultural centre of gravity to the numerous regional centres, Kievan traditions were in the main continued and in some cases (i.e., Galician literature, Novgorodian icon painting, Suzdalian architecture) enjoyed remarkable development.

Nor are notions of stultification and isolation from the West supported. The enormous Novgorodian culture sphere, the upper Dnieper territories that eventually came under Lithuanian control, and the principalities of Volhynia and Galicia all had, if anything, closer contacts with western and central Europe than in the previous period.

In the areas of religion and intellectual life, "Tatar influence" was practically nonexistent due to the control of formal culture by the Orthodox clergy and Muslim divines and the limited contact between the Slavic and Turkic populations. There is no evidence that any single Turkic or Islamic text of religious, philosophical, literary or scholarly content was translated directly into Slavonic or any East Slavic vernacular during the period.

Concerning the secular culture of the court and counting house, the situation was radically different. These spheres were controlled by very pragmatic princes, merchants, and diplomats. There, Slavs and Tatars elaborated together an international subculture whose language was Turkic and whose administrative techniques and chancellery culture were essentially those of the Golden Horde. Slavic merchants took full part in this culture, and the princes of Muscovy in particular developed their original court culture and chancellery practices within its context. These borrowings were not of a theoretical or ideological nature, and ascribing later despotism to "Oriental" influence is inaccurate.

Chapter Two

Rurikid Muscovy

The collapse of the Golden Horde saw a growth in the political power of the old sedentary centres—Muscovy, Lithuania, the Volga Bulgar region (which became the khanate of Kazan), and Crimea. This growth was accompanied by dynastic struggles. This period of recovery also saw cooperation among the emerging dynasties against their internal enemies and toward the stabilization of the steppe.

Even by the end of the 14th century, Moscow's position was by no means as dominating as the cartographers' conventions or the historians' hindsight makes it seem. Other centres—Lithuania, Tver, Novgorod—were as rich and powerful as Moscow. Many of the areas nominally subject to the Muscovite princes retained their own dynasties, whose members often broke away and sided with one of Moscow's rivals. Only after a series of dynastic conflicts in the early 15th century did Moscow emerge as the leader of the Russian territory.

The struggle began at the death of Vasily I, a son of Dmitry Donskoy, in 1425. The succession of his 10-year-old son Vasily II was challenged by his uncle Yury, prince of the important upper Volga commercial town of Galich. After many turns of fortune, Vasily II succeeded, with the help of Lithuanian and Tatar allies, in establishing his house permanently as the rulers of Muscovy.

IVAN III

Ivan III (ruled 1462–1505) consolidated from a secure throne the gains his father, Vasily II, had won. The "gathering of the Russian lands," as it has traditionally been known, became under Ivan a conscious and irresistible drive by Moscow to annex all East Slavic lands, both the Russian territories, which traditionally had close links with Moscow, and the Belarusian and Ukrainian regions, which had developed under distinctly different historical and cultural circumstances. In 1471 Ivan mounted a simultaneous attack upon Novgorod and its upper Volga colonies, which capitulated and accepted Moscow's commercial and political demands. The trading republic, however, retained considerable de facto independence and became involved with the Lithuanian princes in an attempt to resist Moscow. Ivan, using these dealings as a pretext, attacked again, and in 1478 Novgorod was absorbed by Moscow. A Muscovite governor was installed, and 70 Novgorodian boyar families were deported and replaced by members of the Moscow military-service class.

Tver suffered a similar fate. Ivan had agreed with Prince Michael Borisovich to conduct foreign relations in concert and by consultation, but, when the Tverite complained that Ivan was not consulting him on important matters, Ivan attacked him and annexed his lands (1485). By the end of Ivan's reign, there were no Russian princes who dared conduct policies unacceptable to Moscow.

This expansion was enabled by his skillful dealings with the Polish-Lithuanian state, which had expanded down the Dnieper basin and into Slavic territories on the south flank of Moscow. After 1450 competition developed for control of the semi-independent principalities of the Dnieper and upper Donets regions. In the early 1490s some minor East Slavic princes defected from Lithuania to Moscow. The first phase of the conflict, confined to border skirmishes, ended in 1494 with a treaty ceding Vyazma to Moscow and the marriage of Ivan's daughter Yelena to Alexander, grand duke of Lithuania. In 1500, on the initiative of Lithuanian defectors, Ivan's armies seized several border towns, beginning a war that ended somewhat inconclusively in 1503 with a truce extending Ivan's border to the west.

The third major element of Ivan's foreign policy comprised his relations with the various Tatar confeder-

This illustration by Aleksey Kivshenko shows Martha the Mayoress being escorted to Moscow. A wealthy Novgorodian, Martha (or Marfa) became a symbol of Novgorodian resistance against Ivan III.

ations. In the 1470s the Crimean khan Mengli Giray came into increasing conflict with Khan Ahmed of the Golden Horde and hoped to ally with Moscow against Ahmed and Lithuania. Ivan, eager to dissolve the connection between Lithuania and Crimea but not wanting to alienate Ahmed, stalled for time. In 1481, when Ahmed died, Ivan forged an alliance with the Nogays, Mengli Giray, and Kazan.

Ivan faced a number of challenges from within his own family and court. In 1472 his eldest brother, Yury, died childless, and Ivan appropriated his entire estate. This antagonized his brothers Andrey and Boris, whose grievances were further increased by Ivan's refusal to give them a share of conquered Novgorod. In 1480 they rebelled, and only with difficulty were they persuaded to remain loyal. A more serious conflict arose (1497–1502) in the form of an open and murderous struggle among Ivan's relatives for succession to the throne. Ivan had named as his heir his grandson Dmitry, but a group close to Ivan's second wife, Sofia (Zoë) Palaeologus, opposed this. Her son Vasily threatened and perhaps attempted an insurrection, and Ivan was forced to accept Vasily.

Ivan became the first Muscovite ruler to engage in diplomacy with western Europe. He wanted a counterpoise to the Polish-Lithuanian power, while the diplomats of Rome and Vienna were interested in the possibility of flanking the growing Ottoman Empire with a Muscovite-Tatar force. In the 1470s and '80s there was an unprecedented traffic between these capitals and Moscow. It was through these channels that Ivan arranged

This portrait of Ivan III is from André Thenet's La Cosmographie universelle, *which was published in Paris in 1575.*

his marriage to Sofia Palaeologus, a niece of the last Byzantine emperor. Ivan's adoption of the Byzantine political style (e.g., autocracy, state domination of the church, etc.) has been often been credited—though probably incorrectly—to his wife's influence. However the territorial and religious conflicts of the Slavic East and the opportunism of the local magnates disrupted Ivan's overtures to the West and brief rapprochement with Lithuania. The death of Crimean khan Mengli Giray in 1515 worsened Moscow's situation, as the collapse of that alliance opened a new period of chaos and readjustment in the steppe.

Although Ivan's reign was notable for the annexation of the rich Novgorodian provinces and for the establishment of a regular bureaucracy and a land-tenure system, these achievements created new problems for his successors. The system of land grants to military servitors ultimately suppressed the interest of both landlords and tenants in increasing agricultural productivity.

VASILY III

Ivan's son Vasily, who came to the throne in 1505, greatly strengthened the monarchy. He completed the annexation of Russian territories with the absorption of Pskov (1510) and Ryazan (1521) and began the advance into non-Russian territories (Smolensk, 1514). Faced with a continuing Lithuanian war and with the breakdown of his father's Tatar policy, Vasily carefully temporized in order to avoid uniting his enemies. Once he had secured peace in the west, he was able to deal directly with the khan of the Crimean Tatars. In the end, however, much of what Vasily accomplished was undone by his failure as a procreator: divorcing his first wife for her apparent barrenness, he married Yelena Glinskaya, who bore him only two children—the deaf and mute Yury and the sickly Ivan, who was three years old at Vasily's death in 1533.

IVAN IV (THE TERRIBLE)

Vasily had appointed a regency council composed of his most trusted advisers and headed by his wife Yelena, but the grievances created by his limitation of landholders' immunities and his antiboyar policies soon found expression in intrigue and opposition, and the bureaucracy he had relied upon could not function without firm leadership. Although Yelena continued Vasily's policies with some success, on her death, in 1538, various parties of boyars sought to control the state apparatus. A decade of intrigue followed, during which affairs of state, when managed at all, went forward because of the momentum developed by the bureaucracy.

Toward the end of the 1540s, a coalition of Muscovite boyars emerged. Inspired by a common awareness of the needs of the state, they embarked upon a program of reform. The first step was the reestablishment of the monarch—for the first time officially designated a tsar—accomplished through the coronation of the 16-year-old Ivan. Shortly afterward he married Anastasia Romanovna Zakharina of a leading boyar family.

On January 16, 1547, Ivan IV was crowned "tsar and grand prince of all Russia." The title "tsar" was derived from the Latin title "caesar" and was translated by Ivan's contemporaries as "emperor."

Ivan was doubtless a puppet in the hands of the leading politicians long after his coronation. The major reforms of the middle 1550s, which produced a new law code, a new military organization, a reform of local government, and severe restrictions on the powers of hereditary landowners (including the monasteries), were probably the work of the bureaucrats and boyars, their objective being to modernize and standardize the administration of the growing state. The immediate goal was to strengthen the state and military apparatus in connection with major campaigns (the first undertaken in 1547) against the khanate of Kazan and to prepare for the major colonization of the new lands that the conquest and others were expected to secure. Toward the end of the 1550s, Ivan seems to have gained the support of certain groups opposed to these policies and to have seized control of the government. The issue was evidently foreign policy. The

THE *OPRICHNINA*

Ivan established his famous *oprichnina*, an aggregate of territory separated from the rest of the realm and put under his immediate control as crown land, in 1564; this was the device through which he expressed his rejection of the established government. As it was his private domain, a state within the state, he took into it predominantly northern and commercial territories that had enjoyed a special prosperity in preceding decades. Specific towns and districts all over Russia were included in the *oprichnina*, their revenues being assigned to the maintenance of Ivan's new court and household. He established a new, much simplified officialdom and a court composed of sycophants and mercenaries, prone to rule through terror, accompanied by persecution of precisely those groups that had contributed so much to the modernization of the state. As trained statesmen and administrators were replaced by hirelings and cronies, the central government and military organization began to disintegrate. The destructiveness of the *oprichnina* was heightened by Ivan's involvement in the costly and ultimately disastrous Livonian War (1558–83) throughout this period (indeed, some historians have viewed the *oprichnina* as a device for the prosecution of that lengthy war's taxing campaigns). Even before the war ended, Ivan was forced by the utter incompetence of his special *oprichnina* army to reintegrate it (1572) with the regular army and to revert, in theory at least, to the previous institutions of government.

planned conquest of the Volga and steppe region had been delayed in execution, and the Kazan campaigns had been enormously costly. By 1557, when the campaigns against Crimea began, there was much opposition in the highest military circles. Ivan took the dissidents' part and for the first time emerged as an independent figure.

Ivan was a disastrously bad ruler, in part because no one had anticipated that he would rule. His poor health and the mental failings of his brother made it quite natural for the regency and the politicians to ignore him and to neglect his education. In adulthood he contracted an incurable bone disease, from which he sought relief in alcohol and in potions provided by a succession of foreign doctors and quacks. Once he had acquired full power, he set about destroying those who had ruled during the interregnum, as well as the machinery of government they had built up. By the time he died, in 1584, the state that he had wanted to reclaim from its makers was in ruins.

BORIS GODUNOV

Ivan the Terrible had murdered his eldest son, Ivan, in a fit of rage in 1581, and his only surviving legitimate heir, Fyodor, was mentally unfit to succeed him. Boris Godunov, who had capped a rapid rise in court circles with the marriage of his sister Irina to Fyodor, soon emerged as the leading player. Godunov's judicious combination of chicanery, vision, and force disarmed his most dangerous enemies when he proclaimed himself tsar after Fyodor's death in 1598. His policies during Fyodor's reign had been conciliatory, and he had apparently succeeded in repairing much of the damage done to the state in Ivan's time.

He conducted a cautious and generally successful foreign policy: the 20 years of his reign were, except for a short, successful war against Sweden, peaceful. In domestic matters, he returned to the modernizing and standardizing policies of the mid-century. He reorganized the land-tenure system, commerce, and taxation.

However a number of problems remained, including the depopulation of the central Muscovite lands and the discontent among small landholders in the territories recently acquired in the south and southwest. Added to these problems was the continuing opposition of the boyars. Despite these difficulties and widespread famine caused by crop failures in 1601–02, Godunov remained in control of the situation until the appearance of the first False Dmitry, a defrocked monk who had appeared in Poland in 1601 claiming to be the son of Ivan IV. (The

A member of the noble Tatar Saburov-Godunov family that had migrated to Muscovy in the 14th century, Boris Godunov began his career of service in the court of Ivan the Terrible.

true Dmitry had died during an epileptic seizure in 1591.) The False Dmitry found supporters in Poland—notably Jerzy Mniszech, to whose daughter, Maryna, he became engaged. As the impostor moved northeast toward Muscovy, he acquired growing support among the disaffected petty gentry and Cossacks (peasants who had escaped from serfdom to a nomadic life) of the regions through which he passed, and border cities throughout the south opened their gates to him. Godunov's troops easily defeated the ragtag force, which apparently had many secret supporters among Muscovite boyars, but a few weeks later Godunov died. The boyars staged a coup against Godunov's family and declared Dmitry tsar. The pretender entered Moscow in triumph, was crowned, and married Maryna Mniszchówna.

THE TIME OF TROUBLES

In the period from 1606 to 1613, during the so-called Time of Troubles, chaos gripped most of central Muscovy. Muscovite boyars, Polish-Lithuanian-Ukrainian Cossacks, and assorted mobs of adventurers and desperate citizens were among the chief actors. In May 1606 a small-scale revolt supported by popular indignation at the insulting behaviour of Dmitry and his Polish garrison brought the overthrow and murder of the pretender. The boyars gave the crown to Prince Vasily Shuysky, a leader of the revolt against Dmitry, with the understanding that he would respect the special rights and privileges of the boyars. While the new tsar had the support of most boyars and of the northern merchants, he could not end the disorders in the south or the adventures of the Polish and Swedish kings, who used Muscovy as a battlefield in their continuing conflict with each other. In 1608 a number of boyars, led by the Romanovs, went over to a second False Dmitry, who had ridden a wave of discontent from the Cossack south into the centre of Muscovy. A shadow government formed in the village of Tushino, 9 miles (14 km) west of Moscow, in which the boyars and bureaucrats of the Romanov circle took leading posts. It managed to gain Cossack support and to manipulate Dmitry's pretensions while negotiating with the Polish king Sigismund III on terms by which his son Władysław IV might become tsar. Shuysky, in desperation, turned to Sweden for aid, promising territorial concessions along the Swedish-Muscovite border. At this the Polish king invaded Muscovy and besieged Smolensk (September 1609). The Tushino coalition dissolved, and Dmitry withdrew to the south. The position of the Shuysky government deteriorated, and in 1610 the tsar was deserted by his army and his allies. The boyars formed a seven-man provisional government with the aim of installing a Polish tsar. This government proved unable to restore order to the country. A new insurgent army, financed by northern merchants and staffed with Swedish troops, marched on Moscow with the intention of ousting the Polish garrison and of bringing the various Cossack bands under control. It nearly gained Moscow but fell apart because its leadership could make no arrangement with the Cossack leaders. A year later a second force, raised in the same northern cities and supported by Cossacks who had been part of the Tushino camp, was able to take possession of the Kremlin. A call was issued for the election of a new tsar.

SOCIAL AND ECONOMIC CONDITIONS

The social and economic life of the 15th and 16th centuries was dominated by three processes: steady economic growth, mainly from colonization and trade; expansion in the power of the central government; and the encroachment of the nobility upon the lands previously held by the free peasantry, accompanied by the fall of the peasantry to serf status.

In the middle of the 15th century, society and the economy were still organized along traditional lines. The land was sparsely settled. Life for most of the population was simple and probably close to the subsistence level. Serfdom did not yet exist. Most of the peasantry lived on state lands and paid whatever taxes could be extracted from them by their prince or his bailiff.

About 1460, measures were taken to bring the peasantry under more regular control of the state and the landlord. Peasant registration appeared at this time, and also the requirement spread that peasants might renounce the tenancy of the land they were working only at the end of the agricultural cycle, in the week of St. Yury's Day, November 26. (The date in the New Style—or Gregorian calendar, which was adopted in the 1580s by

Catholic Europe, but was not used in Russia until 1918—is December 8). The growing controls upon the peasantry received impetus from the large-scale deportations and colonizations that accompanied the annexations of Novgorod, Tver, Pskov, and Ryazan, when the old nobility were replaced with nobility owing service to the prince of Muscovy. The nationwide promulgation of the restriction on movement to St. Yury's Day was contained in the law code of 1497, which added the stipulation that peasants leaving a former situation must pay the landlord all arrears in addition to a departure fee. All of the measures, together with the expansion of the state apparatus for tax gathering and adjudication of disputes over land and peasants, were associated with the growing complexity and power of the central government.

The law code of 1550 repeated the stipulation of 1497 limiting peasant departure, but with more specific provisions and stronger sanctions. Other reforms put an end to local administration by rotating military governors and limited monastic landholding and the juridical rights of landlords over their peasants. The events and policies of the latter half of the reign of Ivan IV destroyed many of the beneficial results of the reforms. The Livonian War imposed unprecedented burdens upon the taxpaying population and the landowning military caste. The political disruption caused by Ivan's *oprichnina* further undermined the position of the service class and led to the looting of Novgorod and other towns. At the same time, other new trends provided the basis for economic growth:

trade in local and Asian transit goods, organized through Arkhangelsk, primarily by English and Dutch merchants, brought unprecedented wealth and luxury to the court; the opening of Siberia provided additional income; and the extension of Russian agriculture into the steppe promised, for the first time, agricultural prosperity.

CULTURAL TRENDS

This period also saw the crystallization of that complex of forms and ideas that can, for the first time, be identified as Russian culture. There was a gathering and integration of the Novgorodian, Tverite, and Suzdalian cultural traditions. Moscow attracted artists, craftsmen, and learned monks who built the eclectic but "national" churches of Ivan III's otherwise Italianate Kremlin and who wrote the revised national, pro-Muscovite versions of the chronicles that had been kept in Rostov, Ryazan, and Novgorod. The regional traditions were not always easily reconciled. Novgorodian attitudes in particular clashed with those of Muscovy.

The reign of Ivan III saw a marked turning toward the West. Ivan surrounded himself with Italian and Greek diplomats and craftsmen. His palace of 1487, his Kremlin with its Latin inscription over the main gate, and his churches, the original aspect of which has been altered by successive Russifying restorations, were clearly in the Italian style, as contemporary foreign visitors noted. His marriage to Sofia Palaeologus had, in addition to its diplomatic significance, a symbolic function of bringing

An example of the "national" churches built under Ivan III, the tiny Church of the Deposition of the Robe (right) *was built in 1484–86 by craftsmen from Pskov.*

Ivan into the circle of Western princes. Muscovy supposedly regarded itself as the heir of Byzantium and as the spiritual leader of the Orthodox world. It may be that the church leadership, militantly anti-Roman, thought of itself in this light. Ivan and many around him viewed the Byzantine heritage as Western, in contrast to the Ottoman and Tatar world, and were at pains to associate Muscovy with Western traditions and interprincely relations. This striving to be accepted in the Western world marked most of the changes in regalia and style of Ivan's reign, although these were later to be buried in the lore of Muscovite Byzantinism.

Three significant causes can be discerned for the evolution of Muscovite culture in the 16th century. The first was the growth and prosperity of the Russian population, united under a stable and increasingly centralized monarchy, which produced the conditions for the rise of a national culture. The second was the diplomatic and cultural isolation in which Muscovy found itself, particularly in the first half of the 16th century, as a result of hostile relations with increasingly powerful Lithuania and Poland, a cause that, more than any other, brought an end to Ivan III's westward turn and to the revolutionary adjustments of the age of exploration. The third cause was the resolution of church-state relations, in the course of which the church submitted to the power of the princes in politics but gained control over the culture, style, and ideology of the dynasty, producing the peculiar amalgam of nationalistic, autocratic, and Orthodox elements that became the official culture of high Muscovy. This new synthesis was reflected in the great undertakings associated with the name of Metropolitan Makary of Moscow: St. Basil's Cathedral in the Kremlin; the encyclopaedic Menolog, or calendar of months, which contained all the literature, translated and original, permitted to be read in the churches; and the Illustrated Codex, a compilation of East Slavic and Greek chronicles in an official Muscovite version.

CHAPTER THREE

ROMANOV MUSCOVY

The military drive that finally expelled the Poles from Moscow led to the election of Michael (Mikhail Fyodorovich), the 16-year-old son of Fyodor Romanov, as tsar. The composition of the coalition that elected him is not clear, but he evidently represented a compromise between the Cossacks, the boyars (especially the Tushino boyars), and the leaders of the northern army. It would be difficult to imagine circumstances less favourable for the beginning of the reign of the adolescent monarch and a new ruling coalition. The military campaigns had left much of the central and southwestern portions of the country in ruins. In many areas, populations had fled, land lay fallow, and administration was in disarray. Significant portions of the Novgorod, Smolensk, and Ryazan regions were occupied by Swedish and Polish armies and by insurrectionary forces, who threatened to renew hostilities.

MICHAEL

The Romanov government required more than a decade to establish itself politically and to restore economic and social order. Few expected the election of a new tsar (the fourth in eight years) to bring an end to the turmoil. But Michael's election permitted the coalition government to address itself to the problems of reconstruction. Also helpful was the survival of the central bureaucracy; the civil servants in Moscow were ready to restore administrative regularity as soon as political order was established. Fortunately, the new government refrained from involving itself in the Polish-Swedish conflicts, which reached their height at this period. This restraint was a most important element in the success of the 1613 settlement, for the international situation was, if anything, grimmer than the domestic one. Polish-Swedish differences permitted Muscovite diplomats to bring the two countries to separate truces (Sweden, 1617; Poland, 1618); although these left substantial territories under the control of Poland and Sweden, they provided a needed interlude of peace. The Romanov government wisely avoided significant participation in the Thirty Years' War, in which most European states engaged. At the death of the Polish king Sigismund III in 1632, Muscovy made an ill-advised attempt to regain Smolensk that ended in military disaster, but in 1634 it obtained Władysław's formal abjuration of the Polish king's questionable claim to the title of tsar.

Michael I established the Romanov dynasty. Michael was also related to the last tsar of the Rurik dynasty, Fyodor I. His grandfather, Nikita Romanov, was Fyodor's maternal uncle.

After the failure of the Smolensk campaign, the government avoided military involvement with Poland for nearly a generation. It concentrated instead upon the extension and fortification of its southern borders, where the incursions of Crimean Tatars were an impediment to colonization. Moscow, however, was not prepared to go to war with the Ottomans, who were the protectors of the Crimean khan. When the Don Cossacks, Muscovy's clients, captured the critical port of Azov in 1637 and appealed to Moscow for aid in holding off a counterattack, a *zemsky sobor*, or national assembly, decided not to intervene, and the port was lost.

ALEXIS

The reign of Michael's son Alexis (Aleksey Mikhaylovich), whom later generations considered the model of a benevolent tsar, began badly. Like his father, Alexis came to the throne a mere boy. The boyar who controlled the government, Boris Ivanovich Morozov, immediately embarked upon policies that brought the government to the brink of disaster. Morozov cut government salaries; he also introduced a tax on salt and a state monopoly of tobacco, the former causing widespread hardship and discontent and the latter bringing the church's condemnation. At the same time, he alienated boyar groups close to the throne by his interference in his ward's marriage.

Morozov's actions exacerbated an already dangerous situation in the country. The city populations and the service gentry in particular were heavily burdened by taxes and other obligations and were increasingly angry at the growing wealth and power of the ruling clique. During a riot in Moscow in May 1648, a mob surrounded the 19-year-old tsar and demanded the execution of Morozov and the leading officials. Some of the latter were thrown to the mob, and a brief protective exile was arranged for Morozov. Morozov's boyar enemies took control of affairs and carried out a series of reforms. The salt tax and tobacco monopoly were ended, and a commission was established for the drafting of a new law code. Serious disorders continued in the cities of the north, particularly in Pskov and Novgorod, where force was required to reimpose authority.

In Novgorod the principal actor in the government's interest was the metropolitan Nikon, an energetic and authoritarian monk who had made influential friends in Moscow while archimandrite at the Romanov family church and continued to cultivate the tsar and his relations while in Novgorod. In 1652 his solicitations earned him the patriarchate. Tradition has it that Nikon, before accepting the position, demanded a declaration of full obedience in religious and moral matters from the tsar. In the first years of Nikon's tenure, his relations with Alexis and the court were good. The patriarch carried out a number of liturgical and organizational reforms, surrounding himself with an impressive bureaucracy modeled upon the state apparatus. Relations with the tsar became strained in 1658, and, after being publicly snubbed by Alexis, Nikon announced that he was abandoning the patriarchate. He

This portrait of Tsar Alexis of the Romanov dynasty was painted about 1670. It is in the State Historical Museum in Moscow.

later held that he had simply gone into temporary seclusion, but his effective power and influence were at an end.

The main event of Alexis's reign was the annexation of eastern Ukraine. His government had continued the previous policy of avoiding entanglements in the West while expanding eastward but could not resist the opportunity offered in 1654 when Bohdan Khmelnytsky, the leader of a Cossack revolution against Polish rule in Ukraine, appealed to Moscow for help. Moscow accepted his allegiance in return for military assistance and thus became involved in a protracted struggle with Poland and Sweden for the Ukrainian, Belarusian, and Baltic territories. At first the war went well, but the differing objectives of the Ukrainians and Muscovites soon revealed themselves. When Charles X of Sweden entered the fray against Poland, Alexis made peace, in 1656; he feared a strong Sweden as much as a strong Poland. Muscovite forces plunged into war with Sweden for the Estonian, Livonian, and Karelian territories along the Baltic coast. The situation in Ukraine became increasingly confused and dangerous for Moscow, and it was necessary to end the war with Sweden in 1661, even at the cost of yielding, once again, the Baltic coast.

In Ukraine the war took on a new aspect when in 1664 Peter Doroshenko, a new leader, put himself under the protection of the Ottomans. The Turks joined in a number of major military operations, alarming both Poland and Moscow sufficiently to bring them to a truce at Andrusovo (1667). Poland recognized Moscow's control over eastern Ukraine and Kiev, while Moscow yielded the part of Ukraine west of the Dnieper and most of Belarusia.

The peace did not greatly improve the government's position, for the same year saw the beginning of a threatening movement among the Don Cossacks and peasants of the Volga region, led by Stenka Razin, and a political battle within the inner circles at court, caused by the death of Alexis's wife. After two years, Alexis married Nataliya Naryshkina. In 1676, however, Alexis himself died, and Fyodor, a sickly son of his first wife, Mariya Miloslavskaya, succeeded him. A struggle began between the rival Naryshkin and Miloslavsky families. The Naryshkins were exiled, and the Miloslavskys took over. In 1682, however, Fyodor died, and the Naryshkin faction sought to place his half brother Peter on the throne instead of Fyodor's full brother, the ailing Ivan. The elite corps of *streltsy* (a hereditary military caste) revolted and established Ivan's elder sister Sophia as regent.

TRENDS IN THE 17TH CENTURY

Economic reconstruction was slow, particularly in agriculture and in the old central lands, but it was accompanied by a growth of trade and manufacturing. The state revenues profited from the expansion eastward beyond the Urals and southward into the black-soil region. In the north the port of Arkhangelsk handled the export of forest products and semimanufactures (naval stores, potash) to the English and Dutch, and its merchants took a leading role in the early exploitation of Siberia. The government itself became deeply involved in the development of trade and commerce, both through its monopolistic control of certain areas and commodities and by its efforts to build up such strategic industries as metallurgy. The economy grew at unprecedented speed during the 17th century. By 1700 Russia was a leading producer of pig iron and potash, and the economic base on which Peter's military successes were to depend had been firmly established.

The political recovery of the Russian state after the Time of Troubles was largely due to the survival of the central bureaucracy and ruling oligarchy. The lines of subsequent development were determined by the growth, consolidation, and almost unimpeded self-aggrandizement of these groups in the 17th century. The expansion of the bureaucratic apparatus can be measured in various ways. In 1613 there were 22 *prikazy*, or departments; by mid-century there were 80. At the beginning of the period, the jurisdiction of the bureaucracy included primarily fiscal, juridical, and military matters; by the end of the century, it also covered industrial, religious, and cultural life. At the close of the Time of Troubles, the bureaucracy's functions were exercised by leading boyars and professional administrators; by Peter's time the mercantile class, the whole of the nobility, and the clergy had become part of its ubiquitous network. This bureaucracy was the buttress—indeed, the substance—of an absolute monarchy whose prerogatives knew few internal bounds.

The ease with which the extension of central authority overwhelmed all other political and social forces is to be explained by the frailty of local institutions and by the absence of independent ecclesiastical or social authority. The Muscovite administration was extended first into the devastated areas, where local institutions had been swept away, and then into new territories that had no significant political institutions, until it became a standardized and centralized mechanism powered by the colossal wealth generated by its own expansion.

These processes were reflected in the great law code of 1649, the first general codification since 1550, which was to remain the basis of Russian law until 1833. Its articles make clear the realities of Muscovite political practice: the rule of the bureaucrats and the extension of the powers of the state into all spheres of human activity. It was based in large measure upon the accumulated ad hoc decisions of the officials and was intended for their guidance. The code made ecclesiastical affairs a matter of state jurisdiction; it gave legal expression to the practice of serfdom; and it enumerated crimes "of word and deed" against the "Sovereign"—by which were to be understood the state and all its agents.

By the end of the century, only those families that had made new careers in the state apparatus through service as generals, ministers, and ambassadors remained at the apex of society. They were joined by numerous parvenu families that had risen in government service. Particularly striking was the prosperity of the *dyak* class of professional administrators, which had become a closed hereditary estate by a decree of 1640.

During much of the 17th century, the government was run for all practical purposes by high officials in cooperation with relatives and cronies of the reigning tsar. Historians in the 19th century, eager to find constitutional traditions in Russia's past, stressed the role of the *zemsky sobor*—an assembly of dignitaries that from the time of Ivan IV had been called together when matters of crucial importance had to be decided. In the period after 1613 it was in almost continuous session for some years. After 1619, however, the services of these assemblies were no longer required. It is questionable whether they ever had any power beyond that of a crowd of military and administrative leaders. The government summoned them, and the government determined their composition.

CULTURAL LIFE

No period of Russia's cultural history has been as full of change, turmoil, creativity, failure, and sheer destructiveness as the 17th century. Russian society emerged from the Time of Troubles shattered and unsure of itself, disoriented and impoverished. This shaken society was then subject to wrenching social and economic change and strong external influences.

The old culture had been the culture of the monasteries. Art, literature, architecture, and music remained traditional, canonical, and orthodox until the end of the 16th century. The 17th century produced, first among the officials and boyars and later among the merchants and middle classes, a new elite that was increasingly interested in European culture and had mainly secular interests. Yet the government of these same officials and boyars stifled native cultural development, and many of these merchants and nobles were drawn into movements opposed to Westernization.

There were three reasons for this paradoxical development. First, Western culture had reached Muscovy largely through Polish and Roman Catholic mediation, rendering it unacceptable to all but those sophisticated enough to take a very broad view of the events of the Time of Troubles. In the Ukrainian and Belarusian territories, the Polish Counter-Reformation had brought a national cultural revival. The books, ideas, and people flowing from these lands to Muscovy in the 17th century,

THE GREAT SCHISM

The contradictions of the age were reflected in the great schism within the Russian church. The doctrinal debate began over obscure and petty matters of ritual, but larger, unarticulated issues were at stake. Religion after the Time of Troubles had taken two directions, which were at first closely associated: the reformation of religious life (with stress on the pastoral functions of the clergy and the simplification of the liturgy) and the correction and standardization of the canonical books (which had come to vary widely from the Greek originals). The government had at first supported these linked objectives, but the supporters of "Old Russian piety" opposed the reforms as they were officially promulgated. When, in the 1650s, the patriarch Nikon began to enforce the reforms in the parishes, where they had been generally ignored, the discontent developed into a massive religious and regional insurrection. Towns and parishes of the north were riven by warring "old" and "new" bishops. The Old Believers, dissenters who refused to accept Nikon's liturgical reforms imposed upon the Russian Orthodox Church, were either crushed by government force, driven to self-destruction, or reduced to silent resistance.

In the end, the Western secular culture fostered at the court and the new religious culture and education spread by Ukrainians and Belarusians, who came to dominate church life, submerged and displaced the disparate beginnings of a modern synthesis within native matrices and cleared the way for Peter's cultural policies, which erected a Western facade over the ruins of the native traditions.

however, were hardly less suspect than those of Roman Catholic Poland, and, as these "aliens" acquired a dominant position in Muscovite cultural affairs, resentment was added to suspicion.

A second reason was the preponderant role of the church and, later, the state, which took over at last the assets, liabilities, and responsibilities of the ecclesiastical establishment. From 1620, when the patriarch Philaret pronounced an anathema upon "books of Lithuanian imprint" (the only secular books in print for the Russian reader), until the end of the century, when the government turned to imposing Greek and "Lithuanian" (i.e., Ukrainian and Belarusian) views upon a resisting populace, the state and its ecclesiastical adjunct had a repressive influence.

The patriarch Philaret was the father of Tsar Michael I. Exercising both ecclesiastical and political rule in Russia, Philaret reformed church administration and strove to minimize the influence of the Roman Catholic Church.

Finally, indigenous cultural forces were unable to assert themselves. They were physically dispersed, socially diverse, and set at odds by cultural and political disaffection. The development of a vernacular literature, which can be seen in the synthetic "folk songs," pamphlets, tales, and imitations produced for and by the growing educated class, remained a marginal phenomenon. They were unpublished because of the ecclesiastical monopoly of the press, and they were anonymous. The promising experiments of a group of noble writers who worked within the formal Slavonic tradition were ended by exile and repression.

Despite these negative influences, the court itself was a centre of literary and artistic innovation, and many of the leading men of the realm were considered cultured and cosmopolitan by Westerners who knew them.

CHAPTER FOUR

PETER THE GREAT AND HIS SUCCESSORS

The accession of Peter I ushered in and established the social, institutional, and intellectual trends that were to dominate Russia for the next two centuries. Both Russian and Western historians, whatever their evaluation of Peter's reign, have seen it as one of the most formative periods of Russia's history. The seminal nature of the reign owes much to Peter's personality and youth.

PETER'S YOUTH AND EARLY REIGN

The child of his father's second marriage, Peter was pushed into the background by his half brother Fyodor and exiled from the Kremlin during the turbulent years of the regency (1682–89) of his half sister Sophia. He grew up among children of lesser birth, unfettered by court etiquette. Playing at war and organizing his young friends into an effective military force, he could manifest his energy, vitality, and curiosity almost untrammeled.

He also came into close contact with the western Europeans who lived in Moscow; the association kindled his interest in navigation and the mechanical arts—of which he became a skilled practitioner—and gave him the experience of a socially freer and intellectually more stimulating atmosphere than he might otherwise have had. He resolved to introduce this more dynamic and "open" style of life into Russia, a goal he pursued after the overthrow of Sophia in 1689 and that he erected into a policy of state after he became sole ruler following the death of his mother in 1694. (His half brother Ivan V remained co-tsar but played no role and died in 1696.)

Peter's first political aim was to secure Muscovy's southern borders against the threat of raids by Crimean Tatars supported by the Ottoman Empire. For lack of adequate sea power, his initial attempt, in 1695, failed to gain a foothold on the Sea of Azov. Undaunted, Peter built up a navy—becoming the first Russian ruler since early Kievan times to do so—and succeeded in capturing Azov a year later. The experience convinced him of the necessity of extending his own technical knowledge and of securing tools and personnel from the West. To this end Peter traveled to western Europe, something no Muscovite tsar had ever done; he spent almost a year in Holland and England acquiring mechanical and maritime skills, hiring experts in various fields, purchasing books and scientific curiosities, and carrying on diplomatic negotiations for a crusade against the Turks. In the course of negotiations with Poland-Saxony and Denmark, an alliance

A man of original and shrewd intellect, exuberant, courageous, industrious, and iron-willed, Peter I soberly appraised complex and changeable situations so as to uphold consistently the general interests of Russia and his own particular designs.

was formed, not against Turkey but against Sweden. The alliance led to the Second Northern War (1700–21), which became Peter's major concern for almost the remainder of his reign.

The war started inauspiciously for Peter when King Charles XII of Sweden, disembarking suddenly on the eastern coast of the Baltic Sea, inflicted a severe defeat on the Russians before the fortress of Narva (November 1700). Thinking that he had eliminated Russia as a military factor, Charles invaded Poland to force King Augustus II to make peace and to install his own candidate, Stanisław Leszczyński, on the Polish throne (Stanisław I, ruled 1704–09, 1733). In the meantime Peter proceeded to reorganize and equip his troops systematically, while the generals B.P. Sheremetev and A.D. Menshikov gradually conquered the Swedish Baltic provinces of Ingria and Livonia. By terms of the capitulations of Riga and Revel (now Tallinn), Swedish sovereignty was ended and the provinces incorporated into the Russian Empire; the local German landed nobility and urban patriciate were confirmed in their historic corporate privileges. In 1703 Peter laid the foundations of his new capital, St. Petersburg, at the mouth of the Neva River; the site was chosen to secure a firm footing on the Gulf of Finland and to open direct sea access to western Europe.

Having forced Augustus II to withdraw from the war, Charles again turned eastward. Invading Russia in 1708, he decided to first secure Ukraine as a source of supplies and manpower (promised by the Cossack hetman Ivan Stepanovich Mazepa, who had defected from Peter's side) and await reinforcements from the north. These reinforcements, however, were prevented from reaching Charles by Menshikov's victory at Lesnaya in September 1708. After much maneuvering, Charles laid siege to the Ukrainian town of Poltava in the spring of 1709. Peter hastened to relieve the town, and it was before its walls that the crucial battle was fought on June 27 (July 8, New Style), 1709. Russian victory was complete—Charles and Hetman Mazepa barely escaped capture, and the remainder of their troops were taken prisoner when they tried to cross the Dnieper at Perevolochnaya a few days later. Charles took refuge with the Turkish army encamped on the banks of the Prut River. Peter made the mistake of pursuing him into Turkish territory and barely escaped entrapment by the Turks, whom Charles had persuaded to renew war with Russia. With the help of bribery and diplomacy, Peter extricated himself from the trap by signing a peace treaty (July 1711) under which he gave up Azov and promised to dismantle fortresses near the Turkish border.

Charles remained interned in Turkey (he did not escape until 1714), hoping to rebuild a coalition and rejecting all peace proposals. The war dragged on: Augustus II recovered the Polish throne, and Peter consolidated his hold on the Baltic by invading southern Finland. Russia won its first significant naval victory in July 1714 off the Hangö (Gangut) peninsula and raided the Swedish

The Battle of Poltava ended Sweden's status as a major power and marked the beginning of Russian supremacy in eastern Europe. It was fought north and west of Poltava in what is now Ukraine.

mainland. The death of Charles XII (killed accidentally in Norway in 1718, soon after his return from Turkey) led to protracted negotiations (Congress of Åland) that ultimately resulted in the Peace of Nystad (August 30 [September 10, New Style], 1721), under the terms of which Sweden acquiesced to Russian conquests on the eastern coast of the Baltic Sea. Thereafter Russia was the dominant power in the Baltic region, while Sweden rapidly sank to second-rate status.

Russia's acquisition of Ingria and Livonia (and later of Kurland) brought into the empire a new minority: the German elites—urban bourgeoisie and landowning nobility—with their corporate privileges, harsh exploitation of native (Estonian and Latvian) peasantry, and Western culture and administrative practices. Eventually these elites made significant contributions to the imperial administration (military and civil) and helped bring German education, science, and culture to Russian society. From a diplomatic point of view, Peter's triumph over Sweden secured Russia an important voice (enhanced by matrimonial connections) in the affairs of the German states. By the same token, Russia was to be drawn into all the diplomatic and military conflicts that beset western and central Europe throughout the 18th century, most particularly in connection with the rise of Prussian power, the decline of the Ottoman Empire, and the domestic turmoil in Poland. Russia was forced to maintain great military strength, which put a heavy burden on the fiscal, social, and economic development of the empire.

The long war's requirements determined domestic policy as well. Only when victory was in sight could Peter devote his attention to a systematic overhaul of Russia's institutions. The hastiness and brutality of steps taken under the stress of war had an effect on subsequent history. Historians have debated whether Peter's legislation was informed by an overall plan based on more or less clearly formulated theoretical considerations or whether it was merely measures taken to meet emergencies as they occurred. Pragmatic elements predominated, no doubt, over theoretical principles. The intellectual climate and administrative practices of Europe, however, contributed to orient Peter's thinking.

THE PETRINE STATE

Formally, Peter changed the tsardom of Muscovy into the Empire of All Russias, and he himself received the title of emperor from the Senate at the conclusion of the peace with Sweden. Not only did the title identify the new Russia with European political tradition, but it also bespoke the new conception of rulership and of political authority that Peter wanted to implant: that the sovereign emperor was the head of the state and its first servant, not the patrimonial owner of the land and "father" of his subjects (as the tsar had been). Peter stressed the function of his office rather than that of his person and laid the groundwork of a modern system of administration. Institutions and officials were to operate on the basis of set rules, keep regular hours and records, apply laws and regulations dispassionately, and have individual and collective responsibility for their acts. Reality, of course, fell far short of this ideal, because Muscovite traditions and conditions could not be eradicated so rapidly. Furthermore, there was a great shortage of educated and reliable persons imbued with such rationality and efficiency (a problem that bedeviled the imperial government until its end). They were mainly to be found in the military establishment, where officer and noncommissioned ranks acquired the requisite outlook, experience, and values in the army and navy established by Peter.

The changeover from the traditional militia-like military organization to a "European" professional army had been initiated during the reigns of Tsars Michael and Alexis. But it was Peter who gave it the full-fledged "modern" form it retained until the middle of the 19th century. The army—and, for the first time in Russia, the navy as well—was manned by recruits drawn from the peasantry (and other taxable groups) whose service obligation was for 25 years. Recruitment entailed liberation from serf status both for the soldier and all his children born after his recruitment. Eventually this provided a path, however steep and narrow, for lower-class children to follow to join the ranks of petty officialdom and nobility. Submitted to savage discipline, the soldier was isolated from direct contact with the population, and his total commitment was to the state. Drilled in modern battle order and technology, the peasant recruit was forcibly "modernized."

The officer corps was recruited in similar fashion from the landowning service class. The young noble serviceman was called to serve from age 15 until his death or total incapacity. In principle, service was permanent with only rare leaves granted to attend to family and estate matters. Called up individually, the service noble was assigned and transferred at the will of the state. In principle, service nobles were remunerated by regular salary payments, though in the reign of Peter I and for long afterward salaries were paid neither promptly nor fully in cash; officers had to rely on their family estates or special gifts and awards. Starting as soldiers and noncommissioned officers, service nobles were to progress through the ranks on the basis of merit and longevity. Minimum educational standards had to be met by officers and officials, and they came to play

Peter personally cut the beards of his boyars, as shown in this engraving. Old Believers and merchants who insisted on keeping their beards had to pay a special tax, but peasants and the Orthodox clergy were allowed to remain bearded.

a crucial role in both the careers and the social status of the service nobility. The empire's large population, which grew at a rapid rate throughout the century, enabled the government to maintain the largest standing army in Europe. Good generalship and the soldiers' loyalty and resilience, as well as excellent artillery and cavalry, made for a formidable military force that achieved the notable expansion of the empire during the 18th century. The Russian bureaucracy, whose members were often drawn from the military, thus acquired a preference for uniformity and militarism that did not foster respect or concern for the individual needs of the various regions and peoples of the far-flung empire.

In the new administration, performance was to be the major criterion for appointment and promotion. Peter wanted this principle to apply to the highest offices, starting with that of the emperor himself. As a result of his bad experience with his own son, Alexis (who fled abroad, was brought back, and died in prison), Peter decreed in 1722 that every ruler would appoint his own successor. He did not have the opportunity to avail himself of this right, however, and the matter of regular succession remained a source of conflict and instability throughout the 18th century.

Peter's concern for performance lay at the basis of the Table of Ranks (1722), which served as the framework for the careers of all state servants (military, civil, court) until the second half of the 19th century. In it the hierarchy was divided into 14 categories, or ranks; theoretically

THE ROLES OF DIFFERENT SOCIAL CLASSES

The same need for qualified personnel that had brought about the Table of Ranks also determined Peter's policies toward the several social classes of his realm. The traditional obligation of members of all estates to perform service to the state, each according to his way of life (i.e., the nobleman by serving in the army and administration, the peasantry and merchants by paying taxes, the clergy by prayer), was given a modern, rational form by Peter. Paradoxically, the reform helped to transform the traditional estates into castelike groups from which—except in rare instances of clergy and rich merchants—it became impossible to escape. The nobility was most directly affected by the change, not only in Peter's lifetime but under his successors as well. The nobleman's service obligation became lifelong, regular, and permanent. The staffs of military and government institutions were no longer recruited on the basis of regional origin or family ties, but strictly according to the need of the state and the fitness of the individual for the specific task at hand. The serviceman was transferred from one assignment, branch, or locality to another as the state saw fit. The office of heraldry within the Senate kept the service rosters up-to-date and decided on appointments and transfers. It was not easy to break traditional family and clan ties, however. Family connection continued to be a factor in successful service careers, especially if a relative was close to the ruler or was a favourite. On the level of the central government and the court, the struggle between cliques for imperial favour was the major factor in determining policy orientations and appointments to high positions.

one had to begin at the bottom (14th rank) and proceed upward according to merit and seniority. Throughout the 18th century the 8th rank (1st commissioned officer grade) automatically conferred hereditary nobility on those who were not noble by birth. In a sense, therefore, the Table of Ranks opened all offices to merit and thus democratized the service class. But because service was contingent on good preparation (i.e., education), it was accessible only to the few—nobility and clergy—until later in the 18th century.

Peter also introduced single inheritance of real estate (1714), attempting to break the traditional inheritance pattern that had led to the splintering of estates. In so doing he hoped to create a professional service nobility unconnected with the land and totally devoted to the state, but the resistance the law met in its application forced its revocation in 1731. He also required the nobility to be educated as a prerequisite for service. Schooling, whether at home or in an institution, became a feature of the nobleman's way of life. Schooling was a radical innovation, at first resented and resisted; but within a generation it was accepted as a matter of course and became the decisive element in the status and self-image of the nobility.

The peasantry had been enserfed during the 17th century, but the individual peasant had retained his traditional ties to the village commune and to the land that he worked. To prevent tax evasion through the formation of artificial households, Peter introduced a new unit of taxation, the "soul"—a male peasant of working age—

and the lords were made responsible for the collection of the tax assessed on each of their souls. The peasant thus became a mere item on the tax roll who could be moved, sold, or exchanged according to the needs and whims of his master—whether a private landlord, the church, or the state. The serf became practically indistinguishable from a slave.

As befitted a secular-minded autocrat who saw his main task as enlightening and leading his people to "modernity," Peter had little regard for the church. He recognized its value only as an instrument of control and as an agent of modern education. When the patriarch died in 1700, Peter appointed no successor. Finally in 1721 he gave the church a bureaucratic organization: a Holy Synod composed of several appointed hierarchs and a lay representative of the emperor; the latter, called the chief procurator, came to play the dominant role. Ecclesiastical schools turned into closed institutions with a narrowly scholastic curriculum. Membership in the clerical estate became strictly hereditary; the priesthood was transformed into a closed caste of government religious servants cut off from the new secular culture being introduced in Russia and deprived of their traditional moral authority. Both on economic and religious grounds, therefore, the reign of Peter I appeared particularly oppressive to the common people. For many it clearly was the reign of the Antichrist, from which one escaped only through self-immolation (practiced by some of the Old Believers), open rebellion, or flight to the borderlands of the empire.

This engraving shows a conflict between the Old Believers and Peter I in the Palace of Facets. Numbering millions in the 17th century, the Old Believers eventually split into multiple sects, of which several survived into modern times.

Resistance and flight were made possible by Peter's failure to endow the government with effective means of control on the local level. Peter tried to have the officers of the regiments that were garrisoned in the provinces double as local officials, but the experiment failed because of the necessities of war and because regular officers proved incompetent to administer peasants. The attempts at copying Western models were also unsuccessful, for the Russian nobility lacked (and was not allowed to develop) a local corporate organization that could serve as the foundation for local self-government.

Peter concentrated his attention almost entirely on the central administration. To prosecute the war, the Petrine state had to mobilize all the resources of the country and to supervise practically every aspect of national life. This required that the central executive apparatus be extended and organized along functional lines. Peter hoped to accomplish this by replacing the numerous haphazard *prikazy* (administrative departments) with a coherent system of functional and well-ordered colleges (their number fluctuating around 12 in the course of the century). Each college was headed by a board for more effective control; it had authority in a specific area such as foreign affairs, the army, the navy, commerce, mining, finances, justice, and so on. The major problems with this form of organization proved to be the coordination, planning, and supervision of the colleges.

Peter tried to cope with these defects pragmatically through the creation of a Senate, which came to serve as a privy council as well as an institution of supervision and control. In addition, he set up a network of agents (*fiskaly*) who acted as tax inspectors, investigators, and personal representatives of the emperor.

Much reliance was put on the obligation to denounce all would-be violators of imperial orders. Those failing to do so suffered the same punishment as the actual violator, while the informer was rewarded with the property confiscated from the "criminal." Internal security was vested in 1689 in the chancery of the Preobrazhensky Guards, the tsar's own regiment, which became a much-dreaded organ of political police and repression. Under different names the police apparatus remained a permanent feature of the imperial regime. The police were also the instrument of the ruler's personal intervention, an essential function for the preservation of the autocracy as a viable political system.

The needs of war, as well as the desire to modernize Russia, led Peter to promote and expand industry, particularly mining, naval construction, foundries, and the production of glass and textiles. The emperor aimed at maximizing the use of all potential resources of the country to heighten its power and further its people's welfare. These goals were pursued in mercantilist fashion through discriminatory tariffs, state subsidies, and regulation of manufactures. Peter hoped to involve the rich merchants and the nobility in economic enterprise and expansion. As a class, however, the merchants failed to follow his lead. Many were Old Believers who refused to work for what they considered the Antichrist. Nor did Peter's urban legislation provide the townspeople with the incentives and freedom necessary to change them into an entrepreneurial class. In fact, the municipal reforms were simply means to collect taxes and dues. Only a few members of the nobility had the necessary capital to become entrepreneurs, and their time and energies were completely taken up by their service obligations. Nor did Peter provide for the security of property and for the landowner's right to dispose of the mineral, water, and timber resources on his estate. The shortage of capital could be, and in some cases was, overcome by direct government grants. But the equally serious labour shortage was not so easily resolved. Peter permitted the use of servile labour in mines and manufactures, with the result that thousands of peasants were moved and forced to work under unfamiliar conditions, in new places, at very difficult tasks. Resentment ran high and the productivity of this forced labour was very low. Most of the enterprises established in Peter's lifetime did not survive him.

Among the important factors in Russia's economic development under Peter was the building of St. Petersburg on the then inhospitable shores of the Gulf of Finland. Its construction cost an estimated 30,000 lives (lost from disease, undernourishment, and drowning) and engulfed vast sums of public and private money. Nobles who served in the central administration and at court were required to settle in the new city and to build townhouses.

The location of the new capital symbolized the shift in the empire's political, economic, and cultural centre of gravity toward western Europe. Trade and social intercourse with western Europe became easier, and the icebound peripheral ports of what is now Murmansk and of Arkhangelsk were abandoned for the more convenient harbours of Riga, Revel, and the new St. Petersburg. After 1721 Peter also extended the borders of the empire in the south along the Caspian Sea as a result of a successful war against Persia (Treaty of St. Petersburg, 1723).

The changes that made Peter's reign the most seminal in Russian history were transformation in the country's culture and style of life, at least among the service nobility. Foreign observers made much of Peter's

On May 16 (May 27, New Style), 1703, Peter himself laid the foundation stones for the Peter-Paul Fortress on Zayachy Island. This date is taken as the founding date of St. Petersburg.

requirement that the nobility shave off their beards, wear Western clothes, go to dances and parties, and learn to drink coffee. These were only the external marks of more profound changes that in a generation or so were to make the educated Russian nobility members of European polite society. Commoners, especially the peasantry, were not so immediately affected, although by the end of the 18th century most peasants, and all inhabitants of towns, had moved a considerable distance from the values and habits of their 16th- and 17th-century forebears.

Most important of all, perhaps, Peter I's reign marked the beginning of a new period in Russian educational and cultural life. He was the first to introduce secular education on a significant scale and to make it compulsory for all state servants. First, Peter tried to use the church to establish a network of primary schools for all children of the free classes—a plan that failed largely because the clergy were unable to finance and staff schools for secular learning. But the specialized technical schools Peter founded, such as the Naval Academy, struck roots and provided generations of young men with the skills necessary for leadership in a modern army and navy. Although he did not live to see its formal inauguration, Peter also organized the Academy of Sciences as an institution for scholarship, research, and instruction at the higher level. The academy's beginnings were quite modest and its development was not free from difficulties, but at the end of the 18th century it was a leading European centre of science and enlightenment, preparing and guiding Russia's scientific and technological flowering in the 19th century.

PETER I'S SUCCESSORS

Peter's unexpected death in 1725 threw Russia into chaos. Normal and peaceful succession to the throne was thwarted by a combination of biological accidents and palace coups. At Peter's death his chief collaborators, headed by Prince Aleksandr Danilovich Menshikov and assisted by the guard regiments, put on the throne Peter's widow—his second wife, Catherine I, the daughter of a Lithuanian peasant. Quite naturally, Menshikov ruled in her name. Soon, however, he was forced to share his power with other dignitaries of Peter's reign. A Supreme Privy Council was established as the central governing body, displacing the Senate in political influence and administrative significance. Catherine I's death in 1727 reopened the question of succession. Peter's grandson was proclaimed Emperor Peter II by the council. An immature youngster, Peter II fell under the influence of his chamberlain, Prince Ivan Alekseyevich Dolgoruky, whose family obtained a dominant position in the Supreme Privy Council and brought about the disgrace and exile of Menshikov. It looked as if the Dolgorukys would rule in fact because Peter II was to wed the chamberlain's sister, but Peter's sudden death—on the day set for the wedding—crossed the plans of that ambitious family.

ANNA

Under the leadership of Prince Dmitry Golitsyn—the scion of an old Muscovite boyar family who had been prominent official under Peter I—the Supreme Privy Council elected to the throne Anna, dowager duchess of Courland and niece of Peter I (daughter of his co-tsar, Ivan V). Golitsyn tried to circumscribe Anna's power by having her accept a set of conditions that left to the council the decisive voice in all important matters. This move toward oligarchy was foiled by top-level officials (the *generalitet*—i.e., those with the service rank of general or its equivalent), in alliance with the rank-and-file service nobility. While the former wanted to be included in the ruling oligarchy, the latter opposed any limitation on the autocratic power of the sovereign. Indeed, the ordinary service nobles feared that an oligarchy, however broad its

Anna had little interest in government affairs. She relied heavily on her favourite and lover, Ernst Johann Biron, and a small group of German advisers to manage the state.

membership, would shut them off from access to the ruler and thus limit their opportunity to rise in the hierarchy of the Table of Ranks.

Anna relinquished most of her authority to her Baltic German favourite, Ernst Johann Biron, who acquired a reputation for corruption, cruelty, tyranny, and exploitation and who was felt to have set up a police terror that unfairly benefited the Germans in Russia. Recent scholarship suggests that Biron's bad reputation rested on his inflexibility in applying the law and collecting taxes, rather than on malevolence. The Supreme Privy Council was abolished upon Anna's accession in 1730, and the functions of coordination, supervision, and policy planning were vested in a cabinet of ministers composed of three experienced high officials, all Russians.

ELIZABETH

The childless Anna appointed as successor her infant nephew, Ivan Antonovich (Ivan VI), under the regency of his mother, Anna Leopoldovna. Biron at first retained his influence, but was eventually overthrown by Burkhard Christoph, count von Münnich. The continuing domination of a few favourites—many of whom were Germans—displeased the high officials, whose position was threatened by the personal caprices of ruler or favourite, and incensed the rank and file of the service nobility, who could not obtain favours from the sovereign without the approval and help of the favourites. The malcontents banded together around Peter I's daughter Elizabeth, whose easygoing ways had gained her many friends. She was also popular because of her Russian outlook, which she emphasized. With the help of the guard regiments and high officers and the financial support of foreign diplomats (in particular the French envoy), Elizabeth overthrew the infant Ivan VI and the regent Anna Leopoldovna in 1741. Her 20-year reign saw the rise of certain trends and patterns in public life, society, and culture that were to reach their culmination under Catherine the Great. On the political plane, the most significant development was the restoration of the Senate to its earlier function of chief policy-making and supervising body. At the end of her reign, Elizabeth also established a kind of permanent council for planning and coordination—the Special Conference at the Imperial Court.

This 1919 painting by Evgeny Evgenievich Lanceray shows Elizabeth with the guards in the midst of the coup d'état she staged on the night of Nov. 24–25 (Dec. 5–6), 1741.

During this period Peter's administrative reforms began to bear fruit. The Table of Ranks became the framework for a class of servicemen whose lives were devoted to the interests of the state. In principle, entry to this class of officials was open to anyone with the required ability and education, including the sons of priests and non-Russian landowners. In fact, promotion in the Table of Ranks was possible only if the individual's merit and performance were recognized by the ruler or, more likely, by high officials and dignitaries who had access to the ruler. The personal element, bolstered by family and marriage ties, came to play an important role in the formal system of promotion. Most significantly, it determined the makeup of the top echelon of the administrative and military hierarchies (which were interchangeable). This group constituted an almost permanent ruling elite, co-opting its own membership and promoting the interests of the families most directly connected with it. In order to solidify its influence and function, it aimed at bringing as many routine government operations as possible under a system of regulations that would make appeal to the ruler unnecessary. The ruler's autocratic power could not be infringed, however, because his authority was needed not only to settle special cases but also to promote, protect, and reward members of the ruling group and their clients. The greatest threat to the system was the interference or interposition of favourites. To guard against this, the oligarchy entered into an alliance with the rank-and-file service nobles who wanted to join its ranks and could hope to do so with the help of the dignitaries' patronage. This alliance permitted successful palace coups against favourites. The system worked well enough to allow the consolidation of Peter's reforms, some success in foreign policy, and a general increase in the power and wealth of the state, despite the deficiencies of the rulers and their favourites.

The system rested on the availability to all nobles of the minimum education necessary for entrance and promotion in service. As a consequence, cultural policy became a major concern of the government and the nobility alike. The members of the service class demanded that institutions of learning be set up to prepare the nobility for better careers, permitting them to skip the lowest

Elizabeth encouraged the development of education and art, founding Russia's first university (in Moscow) and the Academy of Arts (in St. Petersburg) and building the extravagant Winter Palace (also in St. Petersburg).

ranks. That demand was fulfilled in 1731 with the creation of the Corps of Cadets. In the course of the following decades, the original corps was expanded, and other special institutions for training the nobility were added. General education became accessible to a large stratum of the rank-and-file nobility with the founding of the Moscow State University in 1755, although the lack of automatic preferment for its graduates kept it from being popular among the wealthier nobles until the end of the century. The Corps of Cadets and similar public and private institutions also acted as substitutes for local and family bonds. These schools became the seedbeds for intellectual life, and their students played a leading role in spreading the literature and ideas of western Europe in court circles and in the high society of the capitals.

The service noblemen were also landlords and serf owners. The majority of them, however, were quite poor due to the low productivity of Russian agriculture, absentee management, and the scattered and splintered character of the landholdings. The average small or middling estate yielded only the bare necessities for the survival of the serviceman's family. As long as he remained in service, away from the estate, and without capital, he could do little to improve his property, especially since any change in the agrarian routine would have to be accepted by his peasant-serfs and the noble neighbours among whose lands his own lay scattered in an inextricable patchwork. He thus depended on the ruler for additional income, either in the form of a salary or as grants of land (and serfs). Salaries were not large, were often in kind (furs), and were paid out irregularly. Lands and serfs could be obtained only from the ruler, and most went to favourites, courtiers, or high dignitaries. Service provided the nobleman with some extras, such as uniforms, sometimes lodgings, and—most important—greater accessibility to court, cultural life, and education for his children. Thus, he remained in service and took little direct interest in his estates and serfs.

Elizabeth's chief adviser, Pyotr Shuvalov, had the government grant exclusive privileges and monopolies to some of the nobility, hoping to involve them in the development of mining and manufacturing. Shuvalov also initiated a gradual loosening of state controls over economic life in general. He began to dismantle the system of internal tariffs, so that local trade could develop. He strengthened the landlord's control over all the resources on his estate and gave the nobles the right to distill alcohol.

At the same time, the landlords were obtaining still greater power over their serfs. The full weight of these powers fell on the household serfs, whose number increased because their masters used them as domestics and craftsmen. When noblemen established factories or secured estates in newly conquered border areas, they transferred serfs there without regard for family or village ties. The operation of most estates was, in the absence of the landlord, left to the peasants. This only perpetuated the traditional patterns of agriculture and made the modernization and improvement of agricultural productivity impossible.

Elizabeth's reign witnessed Russian victories over Turkey that expanded and consolidated the empire's control in southwestern Ukraine and promoted settlement there. Moreover, Russia was interfering more and more in the domestic politics of Poland and in the diplomatic game of central and western Europe. Elizabeth joined Austria, France, Sweden, and Saxony in a coalition against Prussia, under Frederick II, Great Britain, and Hanover. This led to Russia's involvement in the Seven Years' War. Russian armies were successful in conquering East Prussia and occupied Berlin briefly. The empress's death saved the king of Prussia from total disaster.

CHAPTER FIVE

CATHERINE THE GREAT

Elizabeth, too, was childless, and the throne passed to the heir she had selected—her nephew the duke von Holstein-Gottorp, who became Peter III. Peter III made himself personally unpopular with St. Petersburg society. He allowed his entourage (mainly his Holstein relatives and German officers) to control the government. The regular hierarchy of officials—particularly the Senate—was pushed into the background. Power passed into the hands of the emperor's favourites, while a modernized police, under the personal control of a general who was one of the emperor's minions, spread its net over the empire. Peter's pro-Prussian foreign and military policy (he abruptly ended Russia's victorious involvement in the Seven Years' War) and his treatment of his wife, Catherine, provoked much resentment. It was easy for Catherine, with the help of the senators, high officials, and officers of the guard regiments (led by her lover Grigory Orlov and his brothers), to overthrow Peter on June 28 (July 9, New

Catherine the Great led her country into full participation in the political and cultural life of Europe, carrying on the work begun by Peter the Great.

Style), 1762. Thus began the long reign of Catherine II, whom her admiring contemporaries named "the Great."

The daughter of a poor German princeling, Catherine had come to Russia at age 15 to be the bride of the heir presumptive, Peter. She matured in an atmosphere of intrigue and struggle for power. She developed her mind by reading contemporary literature, especially the works of the French Encyclopaedists and of German jurists and cameralists. When she seized power at age 33, she was well prepared, as her reign would prove.

Even before seizing power, Catherine wrote that the task of good government was to promote the general welfare of the nation by providing for the security of person and property. To that end, government should operate in a legal and orderly fashion, furthering the interests of individual subjects and giving groups and classes as much autonomy in the pursuit of their normal activities as possible. All the same, Catherine believed that the autocratic state had important functions. She had no intention of relinquishing or limiting her authority, though she was willing to delegate certain tasks to an educated elite.

EXPANSION OF THE EMPIRE

Catherine's reign was notable for imperial expansion. First in importance for the empire were the securing of the northern shore of the Black Sea (Treaty of Küçük Kaynarca, 1774), the annexation of the Crimean Peninsula (1783), and the expansion into the steppes beyond the Urals and along the Caspian Sea. This permitted the adequate protection of Russian agricultural settlements in the south and southeast and the establishment of trade routes through the Black Sea and up the Danube. On the other hand, these gains involved Russia more and more in the political and military struggle over the crumbling Ottoman Empire in the Balkans.

Grigory Aleksandrovich Potemkin, Catherine's favourite in the 1770s, was the chief architect of her imperial policy. He promoted large-scale foreign colonization and peasant resettlement in the south—with only mediocre success so far as agricultural settlements went but with great success in the foundation and rapid growth of such towns and ports as Odessa, Kherson, Nikolayev, Taganrog, and Mariupol (Pavlovsk). Within a generation or two, these became lively cultural centres and major commercial cities for all of southern Russia, contributing to the reorientation of Russia's pattern of trade with the development of agricultural exports from Ukraine. Local society was transformed on the Russian pattern. Landlords became imperial service nobles with full control over their peasants. Vast new lands were parceled out to prominent officials and made available for purchase by wealthy Russian nobles, who also received the right to resettle their own serfs from the central regions. Thus serfdom, along with elements of the plantation system, was extended over whole new provinces. While this expansion benefited the state and a small, wealthy part of the Russian nobility, it increased the misery and exploitation of the Ukrainian and Russian peasantries. The traditional

Potemkin was Catherine's lover for two years and for 17 years the most powerful man in the empire. An able administrator, licentious, extravagant, loyal, generous, and magnanimous, he was the subject of many anecdotes.

military democracies of the Cossack hosts on the Dnieper, Don, Ural, Kuban, and Volga rivers lost their autonomy and special privileges. The wealthier officers became Russian service nobles, receiving the right to own and settle serfs on their own lands, while the rank-and-file Cossacks sank to the level of state peasants with special military obligations.

In the course of the Russo-Turkish War of 1768–74, Frederick II of Prussia suggested that Russia, Austria, and Prussia find territorial compensation at the expense of Poland rather than squabble over the spoils of the Ottoman Empire. The internal situation of the Polish Commonwealth—in particular the treatment of non-Catholics, which allegedly

AN INCREASINGLY DIVERSE RUSSIA

Integration of the new territories required the absorption of a large number of non-Russian, non-Christian nomadic peoples. The approach that prevailed until the late 19th century was based on the idea, taken from Enlightenment writings, that there is a natural progress of society from primitive hunting and fishing groups through the stage of nomadism to settled agriculture, trade, and urbanization. Accordingly, the government sought to bring the nomadic peoples up to what it considered to be the Russian peasantry's higher way of life. This policy had the advantage also of producing uniformity in administrative and legal structures.

Catherine's government was quite willing to let religious, cultural, or linguistic differences stand, although it did not feel committed to protect them actively. Inevitably, however, its effort to change the ways of the nomads affected their culture and religion and, through these, their social equilibrium and sense of national identity. While Catherine's policy led some peoples to accept (more or less under duress) changes in their way of life, thus facilitating the extension of Russian agricultural settlements onto the open steppes, it also gave rise to a growing sense of identity based on cultural, linguistic, and religious traditions. These nationalistic sentiments clashed with the outlook and practices of officials accustomed to thinking in universal categories. The policy thus defeated its own aims: it handicapped the economic development of the empire's border regions (e.g., in Siberia) and worked against the social and cultural integration of the natives into the fold of the dominant Russian culture (although Russification did take place on a significant scale in the case of some native elites, as in the Caucasus and Crimea).

Poland's size was progressively reduced by three territorial divisions (1772, 1793, 1795) perpetrated by Russia, Prussia, and Austria. After the final partition, the state of Poland ceased to exist.

was grossly discriminatory—had led the three neighbours to meddle in Poland's domestic affairs. After much diplomatic and political maneuvering, Russia, Prussia, and Austria compelled Poland to cede large chunks of its territory in the First Partition (1772–73), the major beneficiaries of which were Russia (which obtained the Belarusian lands) and Austria (Prussia obtained less actual territory, but what it acquired was of great economic value). Polish patriots attempted to bring political stability to their country by drafting the "Constitution of 3 May 1791," which provided for stronger royal authority, established four-year sessions of the elected Sejm (the Polish diet), abolished the liberum veto in its proceedings (under the liberum veto, any single member of the Sejm could kill a measure), and introduced significant liberal reforms in education and law. The prospect of social and political progress within the framework of a stable government did not suit the partitioning powers, so the Second Partition was forced on the Poles in 1792. The revolt led by Tadeusz Kościuszko to save Poland's independence was crushed, and in 1795 the three neighbours seized the remainder of the country and ended its political sovereignty and national independence.

In the short term the partitions seemed a significant success for the Russian Empire, completing the "gathering of 'Russian' lands" (begun in the 15th century) with the acquisition of Belarusia and Volyn, but in the long run they proved more of a liability. Russia became politically tied to Prussia and had to shoulder an increased military burden to defend its new boundaries as well as to maintain law and order among a people restive under foreign occupation. It also proved difficult to co-opt the Polish elites into the imperial establishment, as had been the case with the Ukrainians, the Baltic Germans, and non-Slavic natives. In addition, the empire acquired for the first time a large Jewish population. It can be argued that controlling the obstreperous nation resulted in a regime of harsh police supervision and oppressive censorship throughout the empire.

GOVERNMENT ADMINISTRATION UNDER CATHERINE

The reforms of local government carried out by Catherine also contained contradictions. The successors of Peter I had not solved the problem of local administration. St. Petersburg relied on appointed officials, too few in number and much given to abuse and corruption, and on the informal control exercised by individual landowners and village communes. However, a great peasant rebellion led by Yemelyan Ivanovich Pugachov in 1773–74 demonstrated the inadequacy of this system. Taking up suggestions of various officials and mindful of the information offered by the deputies to the Legislative Commission (1767–68), Catherine shaped the local administration into a structure that remained in force until the middle of the 19th century and also served as a foundation for the *zemstvos* (local elected councils), established in 1864. The basic pattern was established by the statute on the provinces of 1775 and complemented by the organization of corporate self-administration contained in the Charters to the Nobility and the Towns (1785). Essentially, the reforms divided the empire's territory into provinces of roughly equal population; the division paid heed to military considerations. Each of these units (*guberniya*) was put under the supervision and responsibility of a governor or governor-general acting in the name of the ruler, with the right of direct communication with him. A governor's chancery was set up along functional lines (paralleling the system of colleges) and subordinated to and supervised by the Senate. The regular provincial administration was assisted by officials who were elected from among the nobility for the countryside and from the higher ranks of townspeople for the cities; these elected officials took care of routine police matters in their jurisdictions, helped to enforce orders received from the central authorities, and assisted in the maintenance of law and the collection of taxes. Other elected personalities (marshals of the nobility and heads of city councils) protected the interests of their respective classes and helped to settle minor conflicts without recourse to regular tribunals. This system multiplied the number of state agents on the local level but also fostered a sense of responsibility among the members of the local upper classes. However, the serfs and the lower classes in the towns had nobody to protect their interests.

Catherine made no fundamental changes in the administration of the central government. The system of colleges was retained, but the authority of the presidents increased at the expense of the boards, initiating an evolution that culminated in the establishment of monocratic ministries in 1802. The Senate supervised all branches of administration, regulating the orderly flow of business. The Senate was also indirectly involved in coordination, mainly because its procurator general, Prince Aleksandr A. Vyazemsky, held the office for a quarter of a century with the full trust of the empress. At the same time, the judicial functions of the Senate as a high court of appeal and administrative review were widened.

The major institutional weakness of the Petrine system remained—namely, the lack of a body to coordinate the jurisdictions and resolve the conflicts of the colleges and to plan policies and control their implementation. A ruler as energetic, hardworking, and intelligent as Catherine could perform these tasks, but with the growing complexity of administration even Catherine felt the need for such a body.

The empire also needed an up-to-date code of laws. The last code, issued in 1649, had become largely inoperative. Peter and his successors had recognized this need by appointing commissions to prepare a new code, but none reached a successful conclusion. Catherine tried to tackle the job, but in a different manner. In 1767 she convoked a commission of representatives elected by all classes except private serfs. For their guidance she drafted an instruction largely inspired by Western political thinkers. Far from providing a blueprint for a liberal code, it emphasized the need for autocracy. In its civil part the instruction owed much to German political philosophy and natural-law jurisprudence, putting the individual's duties before his rights, emphasizing the state's responsibility for the welfare of the nation, and encouraging the pursuit of material self-interest within the established order. Although not implemented by the commission (which was adjourned indefinitely in 1768), the instruction stimulated the modernization of Russian political and legal thought in the early 19th century.

ГОСПОДИ БОЖЕ МОЙ! ВОНМИ МИ, И ВРАЗУМИ МЯ, ДА СОТВОРЮ СУДЪ ЛЮДЕМЪ ТВОИМЪ ПО ЗАКОНУ СВЯТОМУ ТВОЕМУ СУДИТИ ВЪ ПРАВДУ.

Domine Deus mi! exaudi me, et da mihi intelligentiam, vt conſtituam iudicium genti tuae, quo ſecundum legem tuam ſanctam dicatur ei ius.

НАКАЗЪ

КОММИССІИ О СОСТАВЛЕНІИ ПРОЕКТА НОВАГО УЛОЖЕНІЯ.

INSTRVCTIO

Coetui ad condendam ideam noui legum Codicis conuocato, plenaque ad id donato poteſtate.

I.

Законъ Христіанскій научаетъ насъ взаимно дѣлати другъ другу добро, сколько возможно.

I.

Religio Chriſtiana docet nos, vt alter alteri mutuo tantum boni faciamus, quantum quidem in cuiusque noſtrum viribus ſitum eſt.

This copy of the Instruction of Catherine the Great *(*Nakaz Yekateriny Velikoy *in Russian) has the empress's orders to the Legislative Commission of 1767 in both Russian and Latin.*

In her social policy Catherine aimed at steering the nobility toward cultural interests and economic activity so as to reduce their dependence on state service. (They had been freed from compulsory service by Peter III in 1762.) She ordered a general land survey that permanently fixed the boundaries of individual estates, and she granted the nobility the exclusive right to exploit both the subsoil and surface resources of their land and to market the products of their estates and of their serfs' labour. The nobles also obtained a monopoly of ownership of inhabited estates, which in fact restricted ownership of agricultural serfs to the noble class. Catherine hoped to stimulate agricultural expansion and modernization by providing easy credit and by disseminating the latest techniques and achievements of Western agriculture through the Free Economic Society, founded in 1765. She also fostered the nobility's corporate organization. The Charter to the Nobility (1785) gave the corps of nobility in every province the status of a legal entity. The corporation's members gathered periodically in the provincial and district capitals to elect a marshal, who represented their interests before the governor and the ruler himself. They also elected a number of officials to administer welfare institutions for the nobility (schools, orphanages, and so on), to help settle disputes, and to provide guardianships for orphans. The corporate life of the nobility did not develop as well as expected, however. The nobility never became the class it was in Prussia or England, but the charter did foster a sense of class consciousness and afforded legal security to the members and their property. The periodic electoral meetings stimulated social intercourse, led to a livelier cultural life in the provinces, and helped to involve the nobility in local concerns. The charter provided both a framework and the stage for the gradual formation of a "civil society" whose members cultivated interests, activities, and values independent of the state's—a trend that would come to full bloom and manifest itself in the first half of the 19th century.

Turning the nobility's interests toward economic activity brought the return home of many landowners to supervise the operation of their estates. Interested in obtaining greater income, they not only intensified the exploitation of serf labour but also interfered in the traditional routine of the village by attempting to introduce new agricultural techniques. In most cases, this meant increased regimentation of the serfs. The secularization of the lands (estates) of monasteries and episcopal sees in 1764 had brought a considerable amount of land into the possession of the state. To reward her favourites and to encourage the nobility to economic activity, Catherine gave away large tracts with many peasants, who now had to work for ambitious and capricious masters.

Serfdom, which had never been acceptable to the Russian peasant, now became particularly burdensome and unjust. It became even more so since the lord's extensive police powers removed his serfs from the state's protection, and the new local officials enforced strictly the prohibition against appealing to the sovereign for relief. There were also the specific grievances of the Cossacks, whose traditional liberties had been sharply curtailed and their social organization undermined, as well as the discontent of the nomadic peoples forced to accept a new way of life. Peasant misery erupted in rebellion, led by the

An illiterate Don Cossack, Yemelyan Ivanovich Pugachov was the leader of the Pugachov Rebellion, a major Cossack and peasant uprising that took place in Russia in 1773–75.

Cossack Yemelyan Pugachov, that engulfed all of eastern European Russia in 1773–74. The peasant forces captured a number of towns and cities before they were finally defeated by government armies. The revolt demonstrated the inadequacy of local controls and was thus partly responsible for the reform of provincial administration mentioned above. It also brought the educated elite to a new awareness of the profound alienation of the peasantry from the culture of St. Petersburg.

The reign of Catherine II was a period of active town planning and building. The number and size of the urban centres grew slowly but steadily. Along with new cities in the south, many old towns were rebuilt and developed. The renaissance of the old provincial centres was in part due to the administrative reforms of 1775 and 1785, which brought an influx of officials and nobles. Along with them came craftsmen, artisans, and merchants. An act of Peter III that permitted peasants to trade in neighbouring towns without passports or controls at the gates gave impetus to the emergence of a class of small merchants from among the peasantry. This trend received support from the administrative reorganization of the towns and the limited degree of corporate self-administration granted by the Charter to the Towns of 1785.

EDUCATION AND SOCIAL CHANGE IN THE 18TH CENTURY

Secular education had been actively propagated by Peter I. At first it focused on technical subjects—those directly related to the prosecution of war, the building of a navy, and the running of the government. This was also the original emphasis of the Academy of Sciences and the school connected with it. But, as education became the prerequisite for advancement in service and as Western ways of life spread among the upper classes, its focus gradually broadened. There developed a class of nobles who were interested in culture for the sake of their own development, as well as for cutting a good figure in society. Beginning in the 1760s, the demand for western European artistic and cultural works grew in the salons of St. Petersburg. By the 1780s the major classics of European literature had become easily available in translation to any educated person. Private boarding and day schools proliferated, as did the tutors hired by wealthy nobles. The Academy of Sciences took its place among the major academies of Europe. Moscow State University and the chief schools of the military, naval, and civil services had become regular institutions.

There were also ecclesiastical schools. The seminaries and theological academies not only trained future members of the episcopate and officials of the Holy Synod but also staffed government bureaus on the middle and higher levels and produced the first native Russian academics, scholars, and scientists. Russia's lack of professional experts in such fields as jurisprudence, civil and military engineering, astronomy, and geophysics brought a great influx of foreigners. They brought with them French and German philosophy: the metaphysics and epistemology of René Descartes and the natural law doctrines of the German school of Gottfried Leibniz, Samuel, baron von Pufendorf, and Christian, baron von Wolff. These emphasized social obligation and the individual's dependence on the community and laid the foundation for a critique of society. The critique was at first directed against the moral inadequacies of individuals, but it soon broadened into the view that the educated man had an obligation to help others improve themselves. In the Russian context the class most obviously in need of improvement was the peasantry. Moral progress, the argument went, was not possible without material progress. This led to an advocacy of practical philanthropy and social action.

Imported German professionals furthered the dissemination of German Pietism, with its emphasis on spiritual progress and on the need to serve man and the community. Similar tendencies underlay the most influential branch of Freemasonry. The Freemasons devoted themselves to disseminating knowledge, relieving hunger, and caring for orphans and other destitutes. The publisher Nikolay Novikov carried the Pietist and Masonic messages to the public in his satiric journals and periodicals for women and children. The major writers of Catherine II's reign (including the empress herself, who dabbled in journalism and drama) produced satires, fables, and comedies of manners attuned to the belief that moral and spiritual progress would lead to social improvements. A similar approach was noticeable in education, which stressed the development of moral feeling

The Russian writer, philanthropist, and Freemason Nikolay Novikov tried to raise the educational and cultural level of the Russian people. He produced social satires and also founded schools and libraries.

in the conviction that a good heart would guide the well-filled head in the proper direction.

All these intellectual currents combined to awaken among educated Russians a sense of national pride and a feeling that Russia had managed to lift itself to the cultural and political level of a great European state. The educated Russian was no longer a servile and mute slave of the tsars; he had made himself into a gentleman, a man of heart and honour, a "true son of the fatherland," concerned about his compatriots and his country's condition and future.

The response of the empress and her entourage to these intellectual developments was ambivalent. The new sense of national pride enhanced the government's prestige and was in line with Catherine's own aspirations for the nobility. But moral criticism of abuses could easily turn into criticism of Russia's social and political system. The outbreak of the French Revolution in the late 1780s made Catherine II particularly anxious. She felt that large-scale private philanthropic and educational activities without government guidance and control were trespassing on her own prerogatives as an enlightened autocrat. By the end of the 18th century, the ideal of service to the state, which had underlain the Russian nobility's value system, had been transformed into one of service to the people. This meant the elite's separation from the state, which Catherine could not accept. A dramatic illustration of Catherine's concern occurred on the appearance in 1790 of Aleksandr Radishchev's *A Journey from St. Petersburg to Moscow*. In it Radishchev depicted social conditions as he saw them, particularly the dehumanization of the serfs and the corruption of their masters, warning that these threatened the stability of the existing order. Incensed by the book, Catherine had Radishchev arrested and banished to Siberia. He became the first political martyr of the Russian elite; his book and his fate foreshadowed the antagonism between the intelligentsia and the government that was to dominate Russia's history in the 19th century.

CONCLUSION

Catherine died in 1796 and was succeeded by her son Paul. A capricious, somewhat unstable individual, Paul had a passion for military order that conflicted with the basic values of the developing civil society. He felt that the nobility should again become a service class (or withdraw completely into agriculture) and help the ruler implement his reform program, even at the expense of its private interests. In trying to reestablish compulsory state service, he made it more rigid, harsh, and militaristic. He sought to promote the welfare of the serfs, but the manner of his approach—a decree permitting a maximum of three days of labour service per week—was clumsy and high-handed; it did nothing to help the serfs and angered their lords. Paul also wanted to govern with his own minions, disregarding both tradition and the administrative patterns that had developed during his mother's 30-year reign. Paul's hatred of the French Revolution and of everything connected with it led him to impose tight censorship on travel abroad and to prohibit foreign books, fashions, music, and so forth. He thereby earned the enmity of upper society in St. Petersburg. On March 11 (March 23, New Style), 1801, he was murdered by conspirators drawn from high officials, favourites of Catherine, his own military entourage, and officers of the guard regiments. The accession of his son Alexander I inaugurated a new century and a new period in the history of imperial Russia.

GLOSSARY

ANATHEMA Occasioning the severest form of excommunication that formally separated a heretic completely from the Christian church.

AUTOCRACY A government in which one person has unlimited power.

AUTONOMY The power or right of self-government.

BOYAR A member of the upper stratum of medieval Russian society and state administration.

BURGHER An inhabitant of a borough or a town.

CAMERALIST A public administrative servant of continental rulers of the 17th and 18th centuries who was a mercantilist and advocated economic policies tending to strengthen the position of the ruler.

CHAMBERLAIN A chief officer in the household of a sovereign or noble.

CONCESSION Something granted, often grudgingly.

COSSACKS A people dwelling in the northern hinterlands of the Black and Caspian seas. They had a tradition of independence and finally received privileges from the Russian government in return for military services.

DEFECTOR Someone who deserts one cause, party, or country to take up another.

EPISTEMOLOGY The philosophical study of the nature, origin, and limits of human knowledge.

HANSEATIC LEAGUE An organization founded by north German towns and German merchant communities abroad to protect their mutual trading interests.

The league dominated commercial activity in northern Europe from the 13th to the 15th century.

HEGEMONY The social, cultural, ideological, or economic influence exerted by a dominant group.

INTERREGNUM A period between two successive reigns or regimes.

KHAZARS A confederation of Turkic-speaking tribes that in the late 6th century CE established a major commercial empire covering the southeastern section of modern European Russia.

METAPHYSICS The philosophical study whose object is to determine the real nature of things—to determine the meaning, structure, and principles of whatever is insofar as it is.

NATIONALISM Loyalty and devotion to a nation, especially as expressed by praise of one nation above all others and intense concern with promotion of its culture and interests.

OLIGARCHY Government by the few, especially despotic power exercised by a small and privileged group for corrupt or selfish purposes.

PATRIARCH The head of one of various Eastern churches, such as the Russian Orthodox Church.

PASTORAL NOMADS Groups that raise livestock and move about within their established territory to find good pastures for their animals.

RAPPROCHEMENT The establishment of or state of having cordial relations.

REGENCY The rule of a person who governs a kingdom during the minority, absence, or disability of the sovereign

RETINUE The body of retainers or attendants.

SECULAR Not religious or related to religion.

SELF-IMMOLATION A deliberate and willing sacrifice of oneself, sometimes by setting oneself on fire.

SERF A tenant farmer who was bound to a hereditary plot of land and to the will of his landlord.

SOVEREIGNTY Supreme power, especially over a political unit.

STULTIFICATION Becoming ineffective, foolish, or absurdly illogical.

BIBLIOGRAPHY

One historical study of geopolitical aspects is James H. Bater and R.A. French (eds.), *Studies in Russian Historical Geography* (1983). Also helpful is Martin Gilbert, *The Routledge Atlas of Russian History*, 3rd ed. (2002).

Judicious broad surveys of early Russian history include Nicholas V. Riasanovsky, *A History of Russia*, 6th ed. (2000); and Simon Franklin and Jonathan Shepard, *The Emergence of Rus, 750–1200* (1996). The history of Muscovy is chronicled in Robert O. Crummey, *The Formation of Muscovy, 1304–1613* (1987).

J.L.I. Fennell, *Ivan the Great of Moscow* (1962), the most detailed account of Ivan III's reign in English, emphasizes his diplomacy and foreign policy. Biographies of Ivan IV include S.F. Platonov, *Ivan the Terrible* (1974, reissued 1986); Robert Payne and Nikita Romanoff, *Ivan the Terrible* (1975); Ruslan G. Skrynnikov, *Ivan the Terrible* (1981), interesting for its official Soviet interpretation of his place in history; and Benson Bobrick, *Fearful Majesty: The Life and Reign of Ivan the Terrible* (1987).

An interpretative survey with significant treatment of the 18th century is Richard Pipes, *Russia Under the Old Regime*, 2nd ed. (1995). The Petrine period is examined in Paul Bushkovitch, *Peter the Great: The Struggle for Power, 1671–1725* (2001, reissued 2003); and Lindsay Hughes, *Russia in the Age of Peter the Great* (1998, reissued 2000).

Pis'ma i bumagi Imperatora Petra Velikogo, 11 vol. (1887–1964), contains Peter's correspondence as well as valuable documents on Russian history up to 1711. Biographies include M.M. Bogoslovskiĭ, *Petr I*, 5 vol. (1940–48, reissued 1969), a detailed study up to 1700; Ian Grey, *Peter the Great, Emperor of All Russia* (1960); M.S. Anderson, *Peter the Great* (1978); Alex De Jonge, *Fire and Water: A Life of Peter the Great* (1979); Robert K. Massie, *Peter the Great: His Life and World* (1980, reprinted 1991); and Henri Troyat, *Peter the Great* (1987; originally published in French, 1979), a popularized account.

Peter's reign and the reforms he instituted are analyzed in Sergeĭ M. Solov'ev, *Publichnyia chteniia o Petrie Velikom* (1872, reissued 1984), by a famous Russian historian; B.H. Sumner, *Peter the Great and the Emergence of Russia* (1950, reissued 1972); Reinhard Wittram, *Peter I, Czar und Kaiser*, 2 vol. (1964), and *Peter der Grosse: der Eintritt Russlands in die Neuzeit* (1954); Ivan I. Golikov, *Dieianiia Petra Velikago*, 2nd ed., 15 vol. (1837–43), on his reforms; James Cracraft, *The Church Reform of Peter the Great* (1971); Alexander V. Muller (ed. and trans.), *The Spiritual Regulation of Peter the Great*, trans. from Russian (1972); and Evgenii V. Anisimov, *The Reforms of Peter the Great: Progress Through Coercion in Russia* (1993; originally published in Russian, 1989). J.G. Garrard (ed.), *The Eighteenth Century in Russia* (1973), provides a collection of essays on different aspects of the Westernization of Russia. Peter's military campaigns and his role as the founder of the new Russian army are explored in the works of a prominent Soviet historian, Evgeniĭ V. Tarle, *Russkiĭ flot i vneshniaia politika Petra I* (1949), also available in a German translation, *Russisch-englische Beziehungen unter Peter I* (1954), and *Severnaia voĭna i shvedskoe nashestvie na Rossiiu* (1958). Foreign relations are described by Leonid A. Nikiforov, *Russko-angliĭskie otnosheniia pri Petre I* (1950); and B.H. Sumner, *Peter the Great and the Ottoman Empire* (1949, reissued 1965).

Works that put Peter the Great and his reign into historical perspective include Vasili Klyuchevsky, *The Rise of the Romanovs*, trans. and ed. by Liliana Archibald (1970; originally published in Russian, 1912); E.M. Almedingen, *The Romanovs: Three Centuries of an Ill-Fated Dynasty* (1966); John D. Bergamini, *The Tragic Dynasty: A History of the Romanovs* (1969), based on English- and French-language sources; Ian Grey, *The Romanovs: The Rise and Fall of a Dynasty* (1970); and W. Bruce Lincoln, *The Romanovs: Autocrats of All the Russias* (1981).

A critical analysis of the relationship between administration and society in the 18th century is given in John P. LeDonne, *Absolutism and Ruling Class: The Formation of the Russian Political Order*, 1700–1825 (1991).

The reign and person of Catherine II (perhaps better known as Catherine the Great) are analyzed in Isabel De Madariaga, *Russia in the Age of Catherine the Great* (1981, reissued 2002), and *Catherine the Great: A Short History*, 2nd ed. (2002). Philosophical and political thought is presented in Andrzeji Walicki, *A History of Russian Thought: From the Enlightenment to Marxism*, trans. by Hilda Andrews-Rusiecka (1979, reissued 1988; originally published in Polish, 1973).

Mémoires de Catherine II, ed. by Dominique Maroger (1953; Eng. trans. 1955), is of great importance for the history of Catherine's beginnings and for an analysis of her character. This edition is not complete, but it constitutes a choice made among the various versions of the autobiography begun by Catherine; all versions stop very near to the date of her accession to power. Equally important are the *Correspondance of Catherine II with Voltaire* (published in various editions of the complete works of Voltaire, as well as in the Evdokimov edition of the complete works of Catherine II, 1893); the *Correspondance avec le Baron F.M. Grimm* (1774–1796), Grot edition (1878), is interesting for its autobiographical character; Grimm was Catherine's confidant. See also *Lettres d' amour de Catherine II à Potemkine*, Georges Oudard edition (1934), which unfortunately is edited without chronological order.

V.A. Bilbassov, *Geschichte Katharina II*, 3 vol. (1891–93; also published in French as *Histoire de Catherine II*, 1900), is the most important work written about Catherine II, with quotations from many documents of the period; the last volume was banned in Russia under the tsarist regime. Ian Grey, *Catherine the Great: Autocrat and Empress of All Russia* (1961), a remarkable work, is a penetrating analysis of Catherine's character and notably of her relationships with Potemkin. Olga Wormser, *Catherine II* (1957; in French), is particularly interesting for its analysis of the social and cultural situation in Russia. Z. Oldenbourg, *Catherine de Russie* (1964; in French), is a work devoted primarily to the first half of Catherine's life.

INDEX